EDGAR ALLAN POET

JOURNAL #3

Edgar Allan Poet
Journal #3

Los Angeles Edition

Edited by

Apryl Skies & Danny Baker

Edgar & Lenore's Publishing House
13547 Ventura Boulevard
Sherman Oaks, CA 91423

www.EdgarAllanPoet.com

Compilation by Edgar & Lenore's Publishing House © 2015

Library of Congress Cataloging-in-Publication Data

ISBN: 978-0-9854715-7-6
Library of Congress Control Number: 2015910601

Printed in the United States of America

Editing, Arrangement & Cover Design by Apryl Skies & Danny Baker

Photography by Alexis Rhone Fancher

Closing photograph courtesy of Lorraine Perrotta

Dedicated to the memory of
Wanda Coleman and *Scott Wannberg*

Table Of Contents

op
happ

Editors' Acknowledgements

With profound humility, we present this collection of word — a celebration of our great, if not invariably benevolent city. A city of the unquantifiable. It is one of wildly divergent paths of proud visionaries and lowly street poets alike — a stopping point en route to its own birth. Found herein is wordsong of blue heaven, serpentine hiss of mephitic smog and gusting bellow of Los Angeles's very own — she, the (in)famous Santa Ana, equal parts blessing and nemesis, struggling for meter despite volatile Fates of churlish motive. It is moonbeam illumination of this world — our world — an untethered flight of both individual and shared experience. A starstruck lift-off, a rainbow quill dipped in limitless inkwells, lifeblood left in a choppy wake.

Our hope — this collaborative juxtaposition strikes a chord on that canvas of life — undulating fortune, misfortune and observation, witnessed from perches above, within, and below intolerable surface noise. It is the indefinable forever pressing us through galactic boundaries into the prodigiously profound poem that are we — majestic poem that is She. That within belongs to those who have graciously bestowed their unique melody and shared those of beloved groundbreakers now at rest. It belongs to tenders of this landscape, who like butterflies, hover chaotic. They are our phoenixes rising from the deepest of depths so the morrow's sand slows its descent into the finite hourglass of a hopeful generation, too often short on hope.

This journal could not have been possible without the unflinching support and commitment of S.A. Griffin and Richard Modiano. It is of no great discovery to those so fortunate as to have benefited from their decades of acquiring and sharing the golden lessons of the Muse, so as to again pass the torch to those who follow — in turn, completing our art's grand circle which like eternity, has neither beginning nor end.

Finally, the immeasurably generous backing of Austin Straus and Pegarty Long cannot be overstated; nor the unwavering support of Alexis Rhone Fancher whose superb photography adds yet another rich dimension to the depth of the words within. Each and every artist whose contributions to these pages has earned explicit mention. Alas, it would be impossible to denote all those to whom we owe our deepest thanks and respect. We are eternally grateful to you all.

Apryl Skies & Danny Baker – 4/26/2015

Foreword

This is an anthology of Los Angeles poets held together by geography. Los Angeles lies on a hilly coastal plain with the Pacific Ocean as its southern and western boundaries. The city stretches north to the foothills of the Santa Monica Mountains and is bounded by the San Gabriel Mountains to the east. Numerous canyons and valleys also characterize the region, making it an area of diverse climatic conditions. The predominant weather influence is the cool, moist Pacific air, keeping temperatures mild throughout the year. Summers are dry and sunny with most of the rainfall occurring during the winter months, and the Santa Ana winds bring hot, dusty winds of up to 50 miles per hour from the surrounding mountains.

The poems herein are not necessarily about Los Angeles, the styles are not the same — they range from the short lyrical poem of personal travail and personal epiphany to a record of the mind moving, and there is no single theme, making this volume one of diverse poetic sensibilities, as diverse as the microclimates of this city. The works represented are from Los Angeles poets both living and dead, emerging and established, lauded and ignored, and the poems themselves are easy to grasp and slippery, radiantly beautiful and harshly ugly.

Reading this anthology is like traveling the length of Sunset Boulevard. It begins at the Pacific Ocean in the opulent, spectacularly pretty urban utopia of Pacific Palisades that has long been a favorite of celebrities and those with six or seven figure incomes, and turns into Cesar E. Chavez Avenue in Boyle Heights, 22 miles down the road. In between the two you go through Brentwood, Westwood, Bel Air, Beverly Hills, the Sunset Strip, West Hollywood, Hollywood, and Los Feliz, Silver Lake along with several other communities. It is glorious and glamorous in some areas and dirty and dilapidated in others. This anthology is also like taking a ride on Mulholland Drive, a 21-mile long road that follows the ridge line of the Santa Monica Mountains and Hollywood Hills, and has sublime panoramic views. So read these poems of glamour and dirt, anguish and ecstasy, and enjoy the sublime panoramic view of Los Angeles poetry.

Richard Modiano

A Song I Remembered from 1979

when wanda coleman sang that night
every atom in my heart did a do si do
turning its partners round and round
my heart would never be the same again

when wanda coleman sang that night
the music was the truth in every word
the way she gave it all out in every breath
the way breathing would never be the same again

when wanda coleman sang that night
I found a new form of courage
that did not require smoke or drink as
it eased my lonely heart that was barely
surviving a missing adolescence

when wanda coleman sang that night
I forgot about my girlfriend turning tricks
all night long on hollywood blvd. alone
I forgot about how far away I felt from hope
with no idea where I would sleep that night
I missed home and wanted to travel far away
all in the same precious moment of breath
I learned more about fear and love as she spoke
her honest beam of song words into my heart
than I had learned from any source of knowledge
from before that night or any source of knowledge
ever since

when wanda coleman sang that night
I heard the song in the words of her poems
the singing has never stopped
the music has never stopped
it is a song that sings loudest
when I take my most labored breath
as I sing along with the song that comes in words
never to forget the song I heard that night
when wanda coleman sang that night

A. Razor

Wanda Why Aren't You Dead

wanda when are you gonna wear your hair down
wanda. that's a whores's name
wanda why ain't you rich
wanda you know no man in his right mind want a
          ready-made family
why don't you lose weight
wanda why are you so angry
how come your feet are so goddamn big
can't you afford to move out of this hell hole
if i were you were you were you
wanda what is it like being black
i hear you don't like black men
tell me you're ac/dc. tell me you're a nympho. tell me you're
          into chains
wanda i don't think you really mean that
you're joking. girl, you crazy
wanda *what* makes you so angry
wanda i think you need this
wanda you have no humor in you you too serious
wanda i didn't know i was hurting you
that was an accident
wanda i know what you're thinking
wanda i don't think they'll take that off of you

wanda why are you so angry

i'm sorry i didn't remember that that that
that that that was so important to you

wanda you're ALWAYS on the attack

wanda wanda wanda i wonder

why ain't you dead

Wanda Coleman

SOMETHING ABOUT SCOTT WANNBERG

One bit that might be ignored by critics is that
Wannberg should not be recklessly passed-off
As a poet obsessed with movies, because he was,
With great care, infusing his language art with

Cinematic references: mainly, to amplify his
Universal vision and he was never caught in
The trap of self-consciously writing in a poetry
Power structure cynical manner conspiring a

Style, as words were endlessly pouring out of
His pores and on to the page: much the way
Automobile engines use viscosity: the same
Way his poetics involved images derived from

A series of the Montage, the freeze frame, the
Jump cut, the cross-fade: but you will never catch
Wannberg genuflecting in front of the false gods
Of populist affectation.

Michael C Ford

The End Will Be Over As Soon As It Figures Out How To Begin

The end claims it's near,
but it was never adept at gauging distance.
It's calling from a scary dark pay phone
on the side of a mediocre back road.

Don't wait up for me
unless you have the fortitude.
I once visited Fort Itude,
it was easily breached.
Its soldiers were overextended.

The history books cough up blood.
They show videos on the naked backs of scarred men and women.
Some of the videos are quite professional.

Charming faceless men and women come to me
and demand I prepare myself for the golden moment.
I haven't anything resembling gold.
All I can offer is a silver moment.
I give them quarters, nickels, dimes.
Put these in the slot machines of your vision
when your jackpot erupts.
Pour me a good large cup
and I'll partake in the way you feel.

The poets lay themselves down on the streets,
they are the new infrastructure.

The exit signs in the eyes of men and women
are bright red this evening
as Little Red Riding Hood and her wolverine pals
reach out across the abyss
and begin singing We Shall Overcome.

I become minute and ooze quietly through a crack in the final curtain.
Inflation has hit and we put hundred dollar bills on the eyes of the dead.

The end swears it can handle the wheel
but you know its had at least one way too many.
The highway patrol drops down from the clouds,
their lights remind you of your first LSD trip.
They had LPs then
and the dogs growled kind.

The end hopes you will attend its wedding anniversary.
Years ago we all held receipts of promise.
We stood on line at the edge of the cliff

waiting for our partners to choose us.
I become a frayed Keno card.
My numbers blur.
You play me soft; you name me slow.
The pit bosses of hell are shrinking,
doctors cannot ascertain the reason.
A change of diet and climate might be in order.
The end is near, I hear someone mumble.
Holly Near? I ask.

Soon the relief pitcher will thank god for letting him give up 3 runs
in the 10th inning and lose the game for his team.
One tires of athletes thanking god only when they prevail.
If you dance the dance you got to thank god all the time,
even when you lose.

Put your hand on the good book,
the one you read standing up as they repossessed your furniture.
Read your favorite passage,
"He stared through her phone book and the numbers he sought went up in smoke."

The end just had heart palpitations.
The end forgot its PIN number.
Take the ATM machine and shove it.
There are rumors of survival in the recalled wheat germ.
There are new landing strips for the baby UFOs.

Put your unruly head on the soft chopping block,
a Lazee Boy way of being executed.
The condemned man ate a hearty fellow human.
The end will rub its magic balm over your aching history.

Here it comes finally,
turning the corner a little too close,
its dreams are on fire.
I grab the hose and give it full throttle.
None of us really are ready to go just yet.

They got a boisterous new tune on the FM radio renegade station,
it'll need us to translate it
to all our fellow walking wounded.
Put your gun down lover,
the bullets are asleep.

We'll have to sit up and watch the sun come out from hiding.
We'll have to continue to tell each other resonant lies.
The end will be over as soon as it figures out how to begin.

Put your knife away lover,
its blade is rubber
and the street we live on
just got a raise.

listening to Townes Van Zandt, Our Mother the Mountain

Scott Wannberg

While Watching A Biopic On TV

        Mr. Jackson Pollock
you dribbled on your life
like a can of motor oil
viscous and shiny
lubing the rough edges
        of your combustion.

        Framed in a house
of the fantastic, your mechanics
bent tradition, broke treasures
like light bulbs and hearts
breaking over stretcher bars
and tension, supportive but easily
        damaged.

Jerry Garcia

Gabriella

A desert breeze just passed through Los Angeles—
Laden with middle-eastern spices
And fragrant with the nectar of wild desert flowers.
She caressed my face,
Lightly,
Then whispered to my soul.
Then,
As from the tremulous tones of Joshua's horns,
The walls about my spirit
Came tumbling down.

Lynn Manning

POEM FROM THE CAFE WALL

Lady, you ride the winds that roar
        of the enormous sea & wave
        smashed rocks.
dip, sing, glide, soar,
gull-like, gull-winged, great free
        movement of joy, & love, & song,
        nothing hidden.
        naked spraying the twisted
human shore
        with beak, claw, wing of your
        magic gift
& don't care that
        most pick up not all
        the charged beak/wings of
                love
bounce, sing, ride the sun's song,
                        the wind's song.
back to your hawk-gulled eye.
no true song dies.
Lady, my homage & thanks,
        For your gift;
                        my eyes.

Stuart Z. Perkoff

the secrets of each muse

who could paint such angry beauty?
not quite angry and definitely not bitter,
but exacting, dramatic and classical;
this woman sings of Europe before the fall.

Modigliani releases the flow of such softness,
his brush baring the aristocracy of beauty,
long and languorous, a sexual calm in color,
but blunting the elemental edges of each line.

a strange mixture expressed in dichotomy;
a mix of a sunset stroll in the Mediterranean
with cigarette smoke rising in Bohemian shadows.
she cannot be captured without the chains.

the painter required, of course, Egon Schiele;
each stark stroke reveals her sexuality radiant,
battling against death, against cages respectable.
her truth exposed, the lovely flaws of a girl lost.

such beauty caught can never truly convey
three dimensions, the dark corners and closed drawers,
all she fears and all she loves: there are certain dreams,
the secrets of each muse the artist can never betray.

John Lavitt

Selection From *Art Is Love Is God*

I belong to no one
In the mirror of time
        Alone

Burning the poem

Burning her vision

Across time's everlasting man
under god's moon
stilled in the mirror

She comes peeling away the mask
beautiful & sad
beautiful
in the mirror
to live forever
Beautiful

Belonging to no one

Frank T. Rios

The Dance Called La Trini

There's a dance that is like running,
a sprint inside a glance,
a dance that belongs to La Trini.
The body swivels through space and emotions,
through terror times and sweet hugs,
through next-morning regrets and wild lips on skin.
This dance is surrender, a bitter douse of memory,
also honey shimmering across a night sky.

There is a dance called La Trini,
perfect steps in an imperfect world.
She dances and the world is clay in her hands.
She dances and the limbs become liberated & supple.
She dances and it's a flight through the mystery of embraces,
infused by the particular solace of being held
and a strange shame in not knowing how to let go.

There's a dance known only to La Trini,
a secret song in the folds of a battered self,
how in time it becomes nuanced,
with measured moments,
surprising even the dancer.

Some days the dance is a wayward waltz,
an unmannered minuet, yet still a sure glide
into the arms of a partner in rhyme,
a partner synchronized,
whose unsure footing and missteps
finally plummet into line with this love,
this woman, this dance named Trini.

Luis J. Rodriguez

THANK YOU HENRY MANCINI

Thank you Henry Mancini
for all the neon boulevards
and all the city streets
of all the cities
and the jazz
and the poetry
of the downtowns
and the uptowns.

For Sunset Boulevard
in the rain,
Hollywood Boulevard
at twilight,
and Wilshire Boulevard
at dawn.

For the Pacific Coast Highway,
Union Station,
and the view from
Mulholland Drive
both sides;
the San Fernando Valley
and Los Angeles.

For jazz gliding its way
down translucent highways
at one in the morning
through the steam
of car headlights
in the pouring rain.

For making me feel clean
when I was dirty
and for the fantasy
that my life
was somehow better
than it was
and for the romance
when there wasn't any.

For crazy but surprisingly
smooth hung-over mornings
when an all-nighter
should have been painful.

Thank you
for the lengthy warm
Santa Ana summer afternoons
over looking a city
from a dingy apartment
with only the view
and you
to save me…

Thank you Henry Mancini
for those
ephemeral evenings
draped across Hollywood
at midnight
like a ghost town
timeless
glamorous
and still
for the exquisite
and the calm
and for the clean
and regal lift of elegance
on to a stairway of stars
leading to a luxurious
and illustrious world
where nothing earthly
can touch me…

Thank you.

Iris Berry

And Where I'm Going

When we ask someone to be our
friend, do we need an emerald ring
to bind the friendship?
"I know one thing: she has a
banging ass body."
The homeless tent sits half on the street
& half on the sidewalk on Mariposa Ave.,
just south of Sunset. Six suitcases,
large flat screen TV, market basket,
a tree, a bike & a scooter form the
perimeter, much covered by a
green canvas & a blue one. I've seen
three of the young inhabitants, clean
& well dressed -- saw a young man
emerge wearing black pants, white
shirt, black jacket, ride his bike west.

Today, a Saturday, I paid a quarter
each way on the #2 bus to Sunset &
Vine. More young whites than week
nights. How could I at age 16 in
Sidney, Nebraska, ever imagined that
at age 73 I would take a city bus to
Amoeba, buy "Hagar's Song," Charles
Lloyd's & Jason Moran's collaboration.
& that I would be eating couscous
& roast chicken & green peas while
listening to a haunting desert suite?

A trim, finely-dressed, middle-aged
woman carrying 2 bags from Trader
Joe's -- the one at Selma & Vine;
one has a bunch of pink flowers sticking
out. She sits on the front left vertical
seat & puts the bags down. The flowers
stick too far into the aisle. She turns
the bag & the pink flowers point to
her. She rides the bus to Wilton Pl
& departs.

When I was a young man, I sat on the
Bowery & wrote poems about men
& menus & streets. The streets are
still with me. I drive them, walk them,
take city buses. TVs on buses ask
you questions, give facts. I look
at the screen briefly, but soon turn
away to look at people & buildings.

Harry Northup

GNOME, WATCHING
　　for Harry

Roots and vines, my darling, root and vines:
friendships, presents, Mexican tin mirror.
Mandevilla vines spread along our doors,
and kindness means two varieties of parsley.

Sweetheart, those gorgeous, low-cut dresses worn
by celebrities touch my heart -- such effort made just
to show the effort, the heavy work involved in
romance. And my reward? The territory I have
earned -- conglomeration of the accurate:

four specific cacti; white plaster Buddha;
companion gnome; water-stained stone rabbit.
Lyricism and decay: the ground our feet support,
the glue that holds those dresses to the breasts.

Beloved, help me tend this mess as long as
I can turn the pages. The round, tin mirror,
combining sun and moon: Its honesty
reflects my age, more gravel in the soil.

Holly Prado

The Falling Rain Entered the Window of Her Aching Heart

The falling rain entered the window of her aching heart
bringing inner peace and freedom
from daily routine and responsibility

Curled in fetal position on the bed
raindrops splashed artistic patterns
and childhood memories ran across
the playground of the mind

Wind swept voices echoed in her ear
and the long awaited dream of which path
to take on the journey
flickered in cinematic brilliance

Trees were bending
Leaves of thoughts blew through the air
Wind strewn flower petals spawned new ideas
and a rain chant grew with fervor
forming a circle around her heart then body

The falling rain entered the window of her aching heart
bringing inner peace and freedom
from daily routine and responsibility
The falling rain entered the window of her aching heart
The falling rain entered the window
The falling rain entered

James Berkowitz

Dead Red Fox

Briar patch of fur on the down slope
where the wet leaves accumulate
whispering past the Indian mound,
past the three yellow buckeyes

the wet leaves accumulate.
Deciduously guarding the Indian mound
the three yellow buckeyes conjoin
their panoply with the scattered basswood

and decidedly guard the forgotten mound.
I carry a gnarled stick like a rifle
under the bare panoply of white basswood,
prod the remains of burnt sienna

with a gnarled stick carried around like a rifle.
The tired day ends, the dirty river flows
each prodded by the remnants of burnt sienna,
decomposing where the wet leaves accumulate.

Angel Uriel Perales

THE LEAF AND THE BUTTERFLY

It lasted all summer, the dilemma of the leaf and the butterfly. I believe it started with a leaf: yellow, relatively small, probably from a linden tree. Crossing from right to left in front of my windshield, obviously in a descendant diagonal, since leaves fall.

But slowly. So slowly and so randomly, that I erroneously took it for a butterfly, only realizing at the very last glimpse my misunderstanding… Oh, no! It's just a leaf!

That was the crux where my mind got nailed, believe it or not.

As I said, the dilemma occupied me for the entire summer. I kept marveling, day after day, at a confusion of yellow leaves falling and yellow butterflies fluttering, also very frequent a sight. Just about the same size.

It was hard not to be cheated by that superimposing, that double entendre… What's a butterfly, geometrically speaking, but a leaf with a crease in the middle? They work just like an origami caught in two different stages. A crease: there, along the leaf's rib… not that difficult, truly. You fold it, simply following the mark, you press it with your thumbnail and it flies away on its own. The trick is complete.

As much as I tried, as in fact I trained myself for, I could not instantaneously tell the difference. They kept fooling me, both the plant and the insect. Did they know? I doubt it.

Was any sensibility offended, was anything troubled in the order of things if I missed, more than once but in perfect good faith, the identity of those yellow aerial interferences? That I really wanted to know, that perplexed me.

Let me come to the point that truly irritated my consciousness, like a needle pricking my fingertip… was there any proof that a leaf was a leaf and a butterfly a butterfly, if I happened to believe the opposite? Wasn't it a mere case of definition? Aren't insects insects because some of us decided so? Isn't it the same for plant parts? If no one was to witness, did nomenclature matter at all?

Could I merrily call leaves flies and flies indeed leaves, or petals, or candy wraps, being somehow totally right in my blur? Who was going to claim imprecision? Was there any, if nobody declared so?

Clearly I was debating within myself philosophical matters of a simple level, trite arguments on the respective values of language, perception and essence, turned inside out for a million times since the Greek… but in my extreme naivety, especially in the brain splitting heat of that pitiless summer, I was losing my reason, in fact, at a steady pace.

Other questions started urging me, spontaneous, unwanted, following each other in waterfall style. How long does an insect live? How longer is that than a leaf's descending parabola? Couple days versus couple minutes… Does it make a substantial difference? Not considering that a dead leaf can resuscitate, blown up by a sudden whirlpool, even long after it reached the end of its journey…

Has the fact that butterflies move on their own, and leaves don't, any relevance? I admit it does. It is easier to pick up a leaf than to catch a butterfly. Although, truly, I have seen five-year olds successfully pin down whole collections of winged creatures, as well as I have run hopelessly after a single branch, puffed away by capricious winds each time my hand came close. Just a matter of circumstances.

Well, apparently, my complex thoughts attempted to justify an encompassing category, some wide-minded concept, admitting both plants and animals in tolerant society.

Ultimately, the question came down to God and that one can of yellow paint…
That stack of cheap paper squares… Nothing to be thrilled about.
A rainy afternoon, I suppose. Gloomy. He started with a quite simple model. Pendulous. Passive. A little flaccid sometimes. But capable of true abandon.
Then, as I said, he folded it on the central line, he pinched a bit for aerodynamics sake. And the stem became antennae; and a tiny, rudimentary engine (just a thought in the creator's mind) added some curves and some freedom to the still casual trajectory.

A brush stroke with that flashy color, that cocktail of lemon and straw, transparent and tangy… and the entire bulk was kicked down on earth, where it still orbits.
While the Lord is still folding, more sophisticated material, does he? He makes things multicolored now, he makes things unmistakable, things who know what they are or they believe so, things who want to be called by their name.

Toti O'Brien

Birth's Dawn

The rejoice of Papua New Guinea's

virgin soil in its blossom infant years of

spring, where green didn't exist but emerald;

in every fallen leaf that rode the liquid diamond

river, through every wildflower the sun

peaked its gold and made his own.

Sapphire plumage disappeared in heaven's mirrors

Where pearl cloud Pagodas reflect the colors

That the howling wind and birds harmonize.

A plane where light never left and nothing can explain the night.

Juan Cardenas

HAND OF MORNING GLORY

Victorian language of flowers
Love in vain
Awaken each day
Full bloom Morning Glory

Declared a malefactor
Following the dictates
Of the Compendium Maleficarum

Hung from the gallows

Left hand
severed for Glory
To open the doors
I could not

My spirit left to drip out
From my body
to seed the ground

For the coming mandrake
To bring forth my love
My sweet dear soulless
Alraune

Joe Gardner

INVOCATION

lady, i implore you
take my hand
& we will go together
lady
over the land

        i have seen yr face
shining full over the black
mountains, a holy eye in the air
a brite call
a shout of joy
        i give you homage, lady
freely, wholly
        let us walk

lady, the trees stand
clustered in council
like gods / tall
strong. in the distance rain feathers like
black chalk
down the bluebellied sky
over the land

remember my eye, lady, what can i see?
my eye is yr eye
        holy eye
            brite love scream
in the sky

lady, humbly, i beg you
take my hand
guide my eye, lady
over the land
lift my vision
my cloud drunk blood

i want to ride down the feathers of love, lady
to where the rain strikes the fat earth
& mixes
& is mud

Stuart Z. Perkoff

Selection From *Art Is Love Is God*

the poem is blind
by the murdering light
& soft hands

She came all
over me the
joy of her on
me

we celebrated
exchanged gifts
broke each other's finger
& ran to the far corners
of ourselves
waiting

      She   comes
      beautifully
      animal
      color of hair
      flying

I come
out of hiding
no wiser

The poem is…

& I follow
the flowering
blindly

Frank T. Rios

a cappella

there is a page i continue to turn to
where a southern pacific marine layer
dissipates over valley horizon.

angels are imagined, but fall hard
despite such hopeful wings.
there is eye contact over whiskey and wine,
a cappella rendition of a song few have heard.

time releases universal pause,
music is made, art adored, and
poetry perceived in an empty glass
on a lacquered, oak wood bar.

he knows the exact shade of her eyes, she his
she is reminded of clouds
over the slow flame of Leonard Cohen,
blue burn of Coltrane and Armstrong.

a thing of alchemy here in this darkened room,
absorbing the sunshine of each other's bones.

Apryl Skies

You Went Down to the River

The river took you, so we blamed the river.

We pointed with our phones, said, That's it,

that's the river. Naked, the police came

to pat it down, read its rights. The river ran.

We took pictures and followed fast, all but

the barefoot police, who winced and tiptoed.

The river failed the polygraph test, every

way it could: laughed, babbled, changed

its answers. What did Inconclusive mean,

we wanted to know, if not Guilty. The judge

was a painting of mountains and we cheered

because we knew he would hang. We wanted

justice like we wanted Heaven. We wanted

Heaven like we wanted new phones. We didn't

count on a jury of stones; smooth, smooth

stones. Geology says a verdict may take years,

piles of years; we should find a way to pass

the time. We go to the river, sit by the river,

hold hands by the river and sing, but not

of you; there're no good songs about you.

Brendan Constantine

Los Angeles In The Rain
for Elizabeth Wagstaff Williams

I am a sucker for the
beautiful in anything

also an easy mark
for the pain

I revel in it

without question
I knew I wanted to be here
by the time I was 6

my mother would
tell stories about the twisted traffic
& how folks would insert themselves
charging any given inch

the notorious smog
in open conflict with the hungry sun

I was completely taken by the
otherworldliness of it all
couldn't wait as I began
counting down the years

those first three weeks or so
I was here after landing during the
record setting heat of September '78
everything ran:
        my sinuses
        my eyes
        my ass

the choking sky thick
& orange obscuring the
endless sprawl & crawl

I thought that there was something
seriously wrong with me for wanting to
be in such a place
that I was certifiable
had to be

but Los Angeles is a mad love

& something that can never be
truly explained or understood
unless you feel it
live it & somehow
love it

I do my best to
treat her good
like a real lady

it has been a healthy relationship

my punk flower thrives
in this converted desert like a
solid gold Cadillac
top down all the way

but you'll never catch me
bathing in the sun
nor will you see me on the beach
except on days like this
when everything is alive
as the concrete river rages unchecked
towards the open ocean
& the disappointed tourists
gold diggers & surface dwellers
have all gone home to
watch the news & map their way
back to the loins of
wherever it is
their dreams were
born as the furniture music
grinds out their dance

I understand the dark & the light
with my own personal cloud
that follows me everywhere
like a little lost sheep

Los Angeles is the
Mother of Reinvention
& I am a black leather animal
grazing on the spikes
contentedly lost & found
alive inside the
puzzle of her constantly
changing skin

this city gave me
my love
my son
the poem
& is in every word
I shall ever write

I must be one of those
shallow assholes you are
always talking about

thanks for visiting
now go home

have a nice day

S.A. Griffin

THE BUMP

South of Pasadena in the far left lane, just before
heading up the hill alongside Chavez Ravine, a bump
lightly jerks the steering column: the driver's side front wheel
tilts and rocks back down.
                              It doesn't matter how old
or ruined a car I'm driving, this is the only moment
I wouldn't trade: complete foreknowledge would tempt me only if
it were written in poetry too personal for anyone else to understand,
of which this could serve as an intimate example.

The Bump previously appeared in *Carnival* (online)

Bill Mohr

poetry

fascinates vermont avenue lostness bugle fence choice news
languishes within waiting horn choose noise home car
who ever chooses to be who he actually is
we are the holi news we are the lost ones who
constantly find new instruments we are those who
go to church in music

no one owns no one destroys no one fills all the way
house where the fences are tied to garages no one
belongs no one finds no one has lost it
age has always found itself sleeping waiting for the dawn
when reasons believe choices are always
finding new turns

my home has lights love warmth
my home has emotions many my home has stumbles
my home has an altogether lack of finding
itself alone my home wills itself to be
whenever those who belong seek
to shine the most attempts to find
an altogether lack of

music shines with no lights music destroys the altogether lack
of willing to die for heart itself hurts never all time
death consumes want where it never was
never will be nor who destroys will not

altogether listen for doors open men sit men argue
men leave women give men herald wait for opening
the night time hears from dark to light
to find home where it always has been
in heart in time all time has journeys far but within

Harry Northup

LET'S GET LOST

We were in the alley behind his mama's church, taking the long way home
after the Easter Carnival wound down. He'd won me a goldfish in
a round glass bowl. I held it tightly, but the

water splashed out as I walked and the goldfish flopped and floundered. It
was the first day of Daylight Saving and the light lingered on
the houses, played with the trees, their snarled branches high and verdant.

Let's get lost, Eric said. What do you mean? Let's leave, he said. Get out of
        LA.
I'm thinking maybe Topanga but he said no. Really lost. Someplace
like... a new start, he said. San Francisco, maybe. It had been

a tough winter. I'd lost my job at Larry Edmund's Theatrical
Bookshop and got three speeding tickets in as many
        weeks, not to
mention the eviction notice the County Sheriff taped to my front door.
        Who knew my
lover's drunken shotgun blast through my bedroom ceiling would get me banned
from greater Los Feliz? Maybe it was a sign? Walking south on Raymond, we
cut through the park, gave the goldfish a second chance at life, compliments

of a drinking faucet and my bleeding heart. Eric stood behind
me, put his arms around my waist, kissed my neck and shoulders.

People deserve second chances, too, he said.

Alexis Rhone Fancher

Selection From *Art Is Love Is God*

Monk plays broken
as the rain beats
Black fingers

Monk's fingers
Smash inside
Keys pounding bone

Years ago
He sd.
      "if I can
        You can"
falling into midnite
spinning around
before he sat down
coming in on a half note…

      stick **pounds**
      the log
      stick pounds
      the log
he sd.
      before dying
      before anyone knew

      The secret six was in town

Frank T. Rios

The Clark Hotel

Wagon red and pigeon shit grey,
it clings to the soil of Central Avenue
like the last root of a dying tree.
Critically wounded by fire,
its charred bowels spill out into the filthy street.
No historical societies rush to its rescue.
There are no concerts to save The Clark Hotel.

First to let the "Coloreds,"
when the word was in vogue-
the pre-war, "Harlem West" sanctuary
where The Count, and The Duke, and Sammy
put up while they bopped The Avenue!
Where cotton pickers and kitchen mechanics filled the streets,
and had the joints jumpin' 'til dawn!
And The Clark was really swingin'!

But that's history.
The tree was transplanted.
now, only the rotting roots remain:

Harry's Corner--
Site of the six A.M. changing of the guard,
where the nighthawks get their nights capped,
and the earlybirds pluck those first bottles from the wine racks.

The Domino Shack--
Where the bones fall hard against wine soaked tables,
and playing cards cut through cigarette smoke like straight razors;
where Moms got run down by a drunken motorcycle
because the jukebox was screaming so loud that she couldn't hear it coming.

The Clark Hotel--
Where Moms crashed on a raggedy murphy bed
with springs that cried when she was too numb to care;
where naked light bulbs illuminated the latest words of wisdom
scribbled on piss stained walls,
and the carpets were crusty with blood
from trapped rats and voided hypodermics;
where death clung to the skin like sweat,
and nobody gave a damn--
The Clark had history!

Now,
it has nothing.
It stands like some dilapidated whore,
recalling those days of fifty dollar tricks,
fluttering its lashes at the other ruins
along The Avenue.   Lynn Manning

Toast to Los Angeles
after a poem by Wanda Coleman

toast burnt black... too black...civil unrest black

black black...aftermath black...under starless sky

black ………………………….

so I get a dumptruck full of thousand dollar bills

then I back it up to the edge of Compton

right to the ridge of Watts

and I call out into the aftermath

"I'm here to help you...I'm here to help you!"

and a voice calls back out of the burnt toast black:

"help yourself, *white bread!*"

Michael C Ford

They Came Knocking On My Door At 7 A.M.

they had a warrant out for my arrest
"what's your name? where's your identification"
i was half naked so they didn't come inside
figuring they'd caught me mid-fuck
they were right
coitus interruptus LAPD is a drag
i showed 'em alias #3
they said "oh, well where is she??"
i said, "man, she was staying here, but she
hooked up with some niggah and split"
"ok. ok."
they left
i went back into the bedroom
you were naked and still hungry, curious
"what was that all about"
"nothing"
i laughed, took off the rag i was wearing
eased into the sheets next to you
we started fucking again
but things had changed

Wanda Coleman

Heavy Blue Veins: Watts 1959

Heavy blue veins streak across my mother's legs,
Some of them bunched up into dark lumps at her ankles.
Mama periodically bleeds them to relieve the pain.
She carefully cuts the engorged veins with a razor
And drains them into a porcelain-like metal pail
Called a *tina*.
I'm small and all I remember are dreams of blood,
Me drowning in a red sea, blood on sheets, on the walls,
Splashing against the white pail in streams
Out of my mother's ankle.
But they aren't dreams.
It is Mama bleeding—into day, into night.
Bleeding a birth of memory: My mother, my blood,
By the side of the bed, me on the covers,
And her slicing into a black vein
And filling the pail into some dark, forbidding
Red nightmare, which never stops coming,
Never stops pouring,
This memory of Mama and blood and Watts.

Luis J. Rodriguez

The Corner

The corner is the ghetto dream catcher

Dealers turn customers into junkies

Bent spoons being burned to chase that first high again, again, again

Wives giving head so husbands won't feel sick and the beatings could stop

Junkies become thieves and take anything that's not bolted down

The corner's concrete is painted in blood from all the victims it's claimed

Souls on the corner are as dark as the asphalt that runs next to it

OD's, shootings, stabbings and beatings are common on the corner

Some come for a taste and stay for a lifetime dinner

The corner is the ghetto dream catcher

Rolando Ortiz

Selection from *Living in Lotus Land*

XXXVI

The moments no longer matter.

It had been some time since I last saw Hank at the track.
It was one of those majestic autumn afternoons at Santa Anita,
the prominent pearl of the San Gabriel Valley.
A slight slivering chill bit through the tepid air.
The sky was a pale lapis blue, cirrus clouds skated above our heads.
I had just moved offices from downtown to Pasadena.
One of my colleagues had a horse running in the seventh race.
I was invited to join him at the Club House Dining Room
three floors above the finish line.
Two floors up was the Club House bar.
On my way up the stairs there was Hank at the bar
leaning across the counter, joking with a young woman barkeep.
I sauntered over to say hi and offered to cover his tab.
He told me to fuck myself since he just put away his wallet.
He was looking much older than I last remembered.
Older and somewhat frail. He asked who I liked in the Second.
I hadn't made my wager yet and said I was on my way upstairs.
He made a face and muttered something about hoity toity me
and why don't I throw him down a steak—medium rare if you please.
I felt awkward and ill at ease. I assured him I was merely a guest
as membership even then came with a high price tag, required pedigree
and a long waiting list. He started back to the bleachers
with a slight wave of the hand and a suggestion
he'd meet me at the winning booths.

Al's Bar, 305 Hewitt Street downtown Los Angeles, March 14, 1994.
Hank has been dead four days now. A memorial service is underway.
Five or six punk bands headline the day's events.
A former lady friend, mother of his only child
is there to recite some poetry and personal reflections.
Frances Dean Smith spelled affectatiously francEyE
—billygoat whiskers ceremoniously intact on her otherwise female chin.
A riotous crowd overflows the bar and spills out into the street.
A chaos of deafening noise substituting as music rakes across my ears.
The crowd impervious to the fact that Hank preferred Dvorak
and Cèsar Franck. I can hear him whisper from the grave:
"I'm glad I'm dead".

J.R. Phillips

Reluctant to Pray

Motion in the valley,
cars whizzing, a dog sneezes.
People lift arms from table
to mouth, perhaps typing
or talking out loud.
A pilot employs centrifugal force,
lifts aerodynamically into the sky.
Castigliano should be so proud
to deflect his shadow so far down
below upon the ground.
A man resistant to knelt prayer
grimaces at the glow from the sun,
perceives the rotation emanating
from his fixed point of view.
The roustabouts drudge in the wharfs,
in the fields, under flapping carps
or inflexible unrelenting roofs,
or exposed awry to the contingency
of nature, whether aging or buried
and decaying, whether continent
or polyglot in the argot of love.
Soldiers ordered to juggle death and war;
Personal convictions precede dilemmas
of absolutes, trust scatters, reluctancies
creep inside in the form of disinclinations.
This is the basis of all discordant disbelief.
This is dissonance, the distance between
the internal smooth flow of the sandglass
and the eternal wind and water dance.
The skilled remain mute while tasked
with mitigating the state of suffering.
If they do talk, these aggrieved doctors,
priests, judges, journalists, funeral directors,
they embalm their whispers into mummified
whimpers, preserved to be read or analyzed
later, as poet philosophers are prone to do.
Motion continues, Castigliano's Method upholds.

Angel Uriel Perales

The Abyss No. 1

Art is always about change.
Art is always an equilibrated act of destruction and creation.
The artist always destroys a thing to create a thing.

The poet, eschewing canvas or stone, plies his craft
in the intimate arena of the human psyche.
Bypassing the physical senses, the poet writes to the soul.

It is the stone and the canvas of the mind that the poet uses as medium,
ruthlessly tearing away the hidden dogma of the subconscious.
Cracks form in the walls and foundations, pebbles tumble down the mountain,
steam and ash begin to rise, the sea swells.

Teetering on the edge of the abyss,
we feel the solid ground slipping out from under us.
Raw panic tightens our throats.
But before the scream can be loosed,
before terror throws us back in retreat or propels us into the blackness
we find that
the poet has created a new vision
a new dream of truth
a new reality,
and just as the last bit of earth crumbles beneath our feet
we realize –

He has restored to us our wings.

Cindy Weinstein

Ode To My City

alone in the blurred evening
crisp blue skies swallow the tops of flailing buildings

      I could dissipate into this coast
      melt into the murmur of long tired steel

lips vibrating
teeth unfolding

      until my smile
      is a skyscraper stabbing the sweetest horizon

Amanda Gorman

THE RESTORATION

You cannot grieve for that which snags no name.
Without that wounded underbelly, memory
cannot commune. Soon the name your friends
And lovers savor as the firm edge of wistful voice
Will vanish. *God loves you*, say the sermons and *Psalms*

But He doesn't know my name, or yours.
Any of our names. The grief that he remembers
Is how no universe can be immortal,
Not even the one he tried to name,
A word that meant, the miracle of nothingness.

**The Restoration* previously appeared in *Spot Literary Magazine*

Bill Mohr

Someday Our Peace Will Come

one day poetry dropped from the sky
and the animals grew iambic pentameter tails
and the people breathed in stars

one day music dropped from the sky
and the architecture turned symphonic
and the people breathed in harmony

one day memory dropped from the sky
and the past present and future sifted like flour
and the people breathed in wonder

smoke and ash
as distant as two sides of the same coin

Ellyn Maybe

I WAKE UP TO NOTHING
for Scott Wannberg

You disappear.
The world stops
beating.
Dogs bark
in rhythm
with nothing at all.
Like this poem
they feel pointless
but bark anyway.
A small comfort
in the dark.

Carlye Archibeque

In the Gomorrah of Glamour and Gimme All You Can
for Wanda Coleman

Life is
one long madness
in the
Gomorrah of Glamour
and
Gimme All You Can.

We,
the living,
wander between
absolute truth
and the delusions
of cap-teethed,
vacant-eyed madonnas
flashing fistfuls
of nirvanaless dollars.

Ballistic spiritualists
and
C.I.A. operatives
disguised as holy prophets
stand on street corners,
shouting machinated missives;

a perpetuation
of purposeless paranoia
and pointless
preambles of pandemonium;

while
media-hungry whores—
whose body temples
have been desecrated
by gods of addiction—
trick their souls
for another toke
off the cash pipe:

one suck
can bring
15 minutes of fame,
or a
sudden OD on vanity.

Life is
one long crash and burn
in the
Gomorrah of Glamour
and
Gimme All You Can.

Our
aggressions,
obsessions,
denials and denigrations
build the cornerstone
of planned obsolescence;

crying out to the world,
expecting echoes
of salvation,
receiving only
long, unforgivable silences;

trying
to shake off all
the insults and
innuendos
nailed to our bones;

bellyfuls of
brutalities and betrayals
acquired over a lifetime,
fattened up on fatalism,
while myopic optimism
stumbles blindly
down the boulevard
of extremely bad behavior;

where
rapists, tailgaters,
drug pushers, pedophiles,
stalkers, shit talkers,
insomnia addicts
and detritus riders
on the storm
of prefabricated love —
suffering the PTSD
of junkyard LSD —
rain down disease and need

on a
saviorless
City of Angels
where
buried underground
one can find more
serial-killer corpses
than new sources of water—

sometimes
the only thing
that can quench
the thirst
is bloodlust.

Life is
one long sadness
in the
Gomorrah of Glamour
and
Gimme All You Can.

Not even tigers
can guard
this landscape of fading ease.
What were once wings
are now only
clipped eclipses
in fancy clothes.

Nowhere
can be found
sympathy
and a healing tea-leaf reading;

only barbed wire
and indignation,

as
pain and suffering
slip through the cracks
like smoke;
cloud mirrors
that can no longer
look us in the eye.

So quarrelsome
are these days
packing
brass-knuckled troubles;

jacked up
on limited visions
of what were once
so brightly promised tomorrows,

while in defense
we
stand armed
with only aerosol cans
of "I Think I Can"
downgraded to:

"No How, No Way."

Every moment,
the future
looks dimmer.

Life is cheap.

As for death:

if,
by chance,
there's rebirth,

it will only be available
to witness
on a limited basis
through pay per view.

Rich Ferguson

On a Summer Day's Pavement

on a summer day's pavement
it never stops shining
as the sky's flesh ripens
a wound pulsing the horizon
wistful pinks and purples

ants fry on a cement skillet
where torn bright Mary Jane wrappers
roll like the last dusty breath
of an ancient man

a busted fire hydrant douses
the worries of squealing naked children
as sweet jazz dances exotically
over rooftops like a graceful, hungry crow

shadows wither and perish
in the wombs of kitchens flickering warmly
with resurrected stories, hopes, and dreams
retrieved from a hidden ash money tin

night knows no beginning
nor any end
time is light as a blessed wafer
of Eucharist placed on a believer's tongue

clocks are scarred, beaten senseless
with heart palpitations, slap of heel against
concrete double dutch rope
skidding under toes
like slave lovers leaping over a broom

the molasses chime of
'not last night but the night before' trickles
into any crevice, closet, ribcage, and throat

men wade through leaves
for the blushing grassy skirts
of junebugs and laughing women
skirmishing with sweat, love, and light

joy skips on the steps
of inevitable doom
lounges on the darkened roof
of an all too familiar solemn song

on a summer day's pavement
I kiss my shadow goodbye
as she dies on the road
but even she knows that here
on a summer day's pavement
life is just too bright

Amanda Gorman

Sway Along the Exploding Dance Floor of Sometime Love

sway and remember how the bones climb the sky
earth whispered that you were its lover
earth fell hard onto the floor and screamed, help me!
when the music shot itself in the knee
and the damp limo refused to find room for your heart
I still felt the music's arms massage my toxic ways and means

dreams waited while the sirens parted their hair
earth claimed it wanted to wear shorts and show off its invulnerable skin
the dogs rummage for bones of endurance
earth coughed up shrapnel and claimed it was fine

come and sway tonight in the ongoing kinetic
come and bump against the new terrain
wound that is man
house of hate that crumbles beneath trying too much
listen for the light it will lighten your hearing
show off your vulnerable skin
man that is song
when the attempt at love crawls through the foxhole of bluegrass
when the cold rain and rambling snow begin to fog your own seasonal window
remember how to snap your fingers when your heart picks up the tune
when your heart picks up the fire

come on then, sway with me tonight
as the dark kisses our cheek and says
my, you taste ever so good

come on then, and don't fear the capacity for love
because the capacity to hate is easy
and the weather is wondering where we live
and the weather is wondering how we live

Scott Wannberg

Miss Jones

she was the great baby sitter — tall dignified
rich warm brown
we'd scream her name pretend to be endangered
run and hide in mama's clothes closet
she'd search house and yard
get angry and upset when she couldn't find us
we'd pop out laughing while
she scolded us for wolfing

delicately she reported on our bursts into puberty
and experiments in sex

on visits to her home she made us family
after play with her nieces and nephews fed us
the best tuna sandwiches on the planet

love and love always for the only person
to ever comb my thick black kinks
without taking my hair out
in handfuls

i loved her coffee stained teeth flashing gold
her thick british honduras croon
how she always called her lover "Mr."

so pretty inside
there was a joy about her i had to be a woman
to understand

Wanda Coleman

Fevered Shapes
    for Jose Montoya, David Henderson, Pedro Pietri & the first poetry reading I ever
    attended, Fall 1973

I wallowed in a needled-spawned world,
addicted to dope and the crazy life,
and yet there I was—in Berkeley
for my first poetry reading.

I was eighteen—with a bullet, as they say.
Earlier I had flown on a plane for the first time.
Sure I've survived half a dozen gun assaults,
cops knocking me around, ODs,
blades to my neck in jail cells, homeless in dank streets,
and beat downs in barrio brawls—but flying?
That scared me to death.

I sat there in a crowded cafe, not
knowing what to expect. Poetry?
I'd never heard this before. Oh, I
had written lines:
vignettes, images, fears, thoughts.
I didn't know they were poems.

I had no idea what a poem was.

First up on the mic was Jose Montoya,
with Chicano prayers of old *pachucos,*
and strained loves and guitar solos,
and Indian hands in corn flour.

Then David Henderson took the stage,
gleaning urban black streets, racist stares,
Black Panther fury & Southern cooking.

Finally, Pedro Pietri came up—Nuyorican
word meister, flashing El Barrio's experiences
with poems located in phone booths & real life wisdoms
that made us laugh and shake our heads.

I had never heard words spoken this way,
more music than talk,
more fevered shapes than sentences,
more Che and Malcolm than Shakespeare.

These poems came for me,
lassoed my throat,

demanded my life's savings,
taking me for a sunset ride,
knocking me to the dust.

These poems were graffiti scrawls
along the alleys & trash-strewn tunnels of my body,
the metaphoric methadone for the heroin hurling
through my bloodstream, the lifeline I already had inside
and didn't know.

These poems were pool sticks, darkened gangways,
a swirl of sunrise after the graveyard shift,
a blood-black yelling behind torn curtains,
a child screaming and nobody coming to help.

They were a women's scent after a night
of lovemaking, a sweet touch of hand to face,
a forest of hair on a pillow,
a moan during an elongated kiss.

These poems were shadowed intents,
startled doubts, sorrows without grief,
the moon without sky,
unknown melodies…
the falling inside that happens
when you push razor onto wrist.

They came for me as I sank into my suicide,
while fidgeting in a chair,
inching under the skin,
as I wondered why I even came.

Jose, David, and Pedro
—I was never the same after this.
They came for me and I've never let go.
They came for me and I've perspired poems
ever since. They came for me—and all my addictions,
my sorry-ass lies, my falling masks,
my pissed-off wives, neglected children,
angry friends, and back-to-back failures
could never, ever, take them away.

Luis J. Rodriguez

One-Day Road Trip with the Man from Now

Any self-respecting road trip
begins and ends with Scott Wannberg.
The moment your foot leaves the ground
and the door slams shut, Scott is your copilot.
Here is what happens
when you hit the road with Scott:
everything becomes Scott. Everything.
I jive you not.

Scott Wannberg *is* the highway,
ladies and gentlemen.
He is the third Thomas Brother.
Watch what engenders when
the road unfurls before you.
Surely you see the anti-grid
of Scott's body. Each foot of concrete
passing beneath Scott's shotgun seat
transforms, revealing wildly new
expanses of earth skin. This man
is the lateral yaw of California.

Watch how the world turns extra friendly
when Scott is the navigator.
See the happy, blaze-vested
Caltrans workers wave at Scott,
then erupt into gorgeous golden poppies
(the state flower of California!)
when Scott waves back.
See Christo plant his yellow umbrellas
like prospector's claims into the sheer walls
of the Los Padres. See how they become
cantilevered suns when Scott say-heys
and points to them.

See the CHP flank us like pilot fish
to follow Scott's jolly lead over the Grapevine
due north through the primordial valley,
past longhorn steer, farmhouse egg palaces,
Armenians in the sun, grapes and cherries
waving from their beds like good children.
Behind us, those mountains lean mossward.
Good bye Scott! Don't forget to send a postcard!
We get, we get, we just get
that you're one of us in disguise,
you one-man poetry volcano, you!

I tie off stems in my mouth
and leave them in a row
on the dashboard of love.
One! Two! Three! for you, Scott,
little knots of my appreciation,
vegetable keepsakes of
what you bring to the vernacular.
Follow Scott's insane map
of varicose trails.
Sing the State. Sing the rest stops.
Sing the most wanted
and missing persons bulletins,
posted and jaundicing at the rest stops.
Sing the mystery of Phillip Taylor Kramer.
Sing the deranged webs of black widows
nesting below the county map boards.
Sing the yowls of dogs free
from the Winnebagos
for half an hour
because Scott sings for them.

Return to the Hockney blitz
down fabled desert fareways,
the desert bending over backwards on itself.
Scott becomes Polaroids and paint jitters.
He plays VW bingo with the Joshua trees
and pear blossoms.
He bestows fabulous T-shirts of concrete
to the scorpion and the rattler.
Scott is every critter's friend.

Along the coast highway
we are low on petrol, but what me worry
with Scott who conjures glittering orange
schools of garibaldi —the state fish!
We coast on the sheer joy of his speech
all the way to the Golden Gate.
And have I mentioned?
Have I mentioned,
O lead-footed compadre,
that this whole, non-stop to Eureka hop
has thus far been done entirely in reverse gear?

Amélie Frank

Bulletins From The Lava Floor: In Remembrance of Wanda Coleman

Wanda Coleman rose to poetic heights by inching her way up through a tense volcano kingdom. And what is this volcano kingdom? America, with its institutional apartheid as its one parenthetical, and as its other, concretized by Brown and Black Watts and the general vicinity that includes South-Central Los Angeles. The latter dimension always a spark away from eruption. Within this irruptive immensity her odyssey began as a 5 year old poet, who, by 13, had published her first poems in a local newspaper..." Quite an accomplishment for an adolescent facing the double pressures of color and gender, while being schooled in institutions she considered "dehumanizing."

Wanda was an exotic, a precocious mantle piece to be observed from afar; her works, bulletins from the lava floor. Tested not only by rejection from the European literary mean, but also by her peers for being odd and out of place. I do not cast these lines as an institutional outsider who has studied maps of the region and dug up its footnotes. We shared the same community as burgeoning writers scorched by its double acidity. Wanda and I have discussed these tensions on more than one occasion. But let me say, it was Wanda who blazed the way, striding unbowed through misunderstanding. Never conversant with the calculated, with the safety of the pre-conceived, she shocked the claw of racism forcing its retreat, scorching it with the hot barbed wire of her language. Not measures one associates with careerism, or with the ploys of a specially pampered marionette skillful at catering to consensus comfort levels. She was dangerous. One could never figure her angle of attack. Not unlike Amiri Baraka, she would aim at unsuspecting targets, be they Maya Angelou, or Derrick Walcott, or draw raised eyebrows from members of the original support group who surrounded Angela Davis.

In this sense Wanda Coleman can never be reduced to a reductive local entity, to be divided up for those too fearful to roam. She took on the urgency of each circumstance, never shirking confrontation with difficulty or discomfort, all the while suffering the sting of chronic poverty. She was never delimited by the provincial psyche that sought her blessing so as to foment its own ineptitude.

We are facing a future which has no place for this, as our species continues to hurtle down an apocalyptic causeway.

Wanda, we love you, we will always love you, knowing that you knew, that the implacable power of language smolders, erupts, precociously igniting a scale of revelation.

Will Alexander

Untitled

let me take my city into my wounds
slashed by lumined jewels of sand
that glow & sting their songs & wings
into our flesh made soft by blood & rot & lice

let me take my city into my hand
my flesh-whipped, fluttering hand, not gull
not even claw of flight
to hold as close as winds under the enveloping wing

let me ride the wing of wind that sings
the erupted earth into the air
the still wing, pierced, trembling
that climbs from slab to slab of stone step, sky

feed my city to me in the flesh
explosion of our joyous flesh
flying my city to my eternal touch
as we, & it, sing the gull triumph
of our rage
& our joy

Stuart Z. Perkoff

In A Park Of Echoes

scorched earth daydreams
trample sacred tongues
into mortal remains
barely standing

the sound of songs sung out loud
echoes off of the brick tenement walls
into the empty parking lot
of last goodbye times

cockroaches scurry down the boulevard
past doorways that open into lost hearts
they never saw this coming in their worst
slash & burn sexual affairs that lacked
enough cigarettes to leave lipstick on butts

the small body of water is still unequal to the amount
of teardrops that fall in a long night time of regrets
that linger in the frets like broken guitar strings
dangling happiness like baited hooks for
wild spiderfish come crawling for victims
to drag back down into the darkest part
of the shallow waters near the boathouse

statuesque beauty honors the upward spray of fountains by
standing guard on the last glimmers of neon twilight that
border the windows of the last taco truck stand off looking
out into the shadows that cast fires against the hills

the fires never go out here or lose control of their heat
the water never clears away the dust from the corners
the air never stays clean enough to breathe in at last gasp
the earth carries the burden of progress while ancient law
sways the palm trees into a motion that keeps the bats from
sleeping tonight among the fronds

over & over again
rippling
then
returning
once more

A. Razor

Highland Park is

Highland Park is sycamore trees, ficus trees, oak trees and palm trees providing homes for the numerous birds that reside here, like those loud parrots in the morning, the eager red tail hawks that circle above your heard, the black crows and ravens or the barn owls that screech at night. Highland Park is bridle trails, railroad tracks, the Santa Fe Bridge, bus lines, bicycles and taco trucks. Highland Park is an artist's haven, rich with color and inspiration. Highland Park is running barefoot in the Arroyo Seco and exploring the storm drains that empty into a river that never sleeps. Highland Park is the Arroyo Seco Parkway, the first freeway in the United States with exits reduced to speeds of 5 mph, drivers beware. Highland Park is home to the most beautiful women in town as expressed by my husband. Highland Park is hip, trendy, tranquil and passive with Abuelitas who sweep up after us on the stained sidewalks. Highland Park blooms with murals that tell our historic stories. Highland Park is Fidel's vs. Folliero's Pizza even though longtime residents will say it's "Luigi's all the way." Highland Park is diverse, wealthy and strong. Highland Park is river rock walls bordering 100 year old homes. Highland Park is old Los Angeles. Highland Park is the new Los Angeles. Highland Park is constantly changing. Highland Park always stays the same. Highland Park is embedded in my memories of rollerskating along Figueroa as a little girl and will always live in my heart.

Annette Cruz

THE KNIGHT RIDES SLOWLY
THROUGH THE GREEN WOOD

to sit in this cluttered room all morning long
1984 Los Angeles summer hot and not a poem in sight
only chair fan ashtray pencils in a cup
cartons in a corner who remembers what's in them?
Venice out the window buildings beaches airplanes
gangs and ghetto blasters mothers all the children
what a time to want to write a poem
nothing comes of course no poem only useless lines
and God knows where they came from:
"the knight rides slowly through the green wood" and
"the sad knight rides through the forest"
just these two lines over and over again
and I write them down and I cross them out
and write them down again
"the knight rides slowly through the green wood"
"the sad knight rides through the forest"
there'll be no poem today just the sad rider
but if sad he is strong he is steadfast
and he rides through the morning in the mind until
the room and the world back off a bit
my nose fills with forest smells
of moss and water mushrooms wild witch hazel
I had hoped for a poem but witch hazel?
I never expected witch hazel and I tell myself
some days most days the thing to do is
to fail and gladly choose the failure
the knight rides slowly through the green wood
the sad knight rides through the forest

John Thomas

Untitled
handwritten poem, taken off Stuart's wall 6/27/74

so black, The visions. That's why they
linked gaunted arms & stumbled towards
the flames in a feeble dance of celeb-
rations. For the visions cannot be
denied, reality is irrevocable &
so, precisely *there* they found joy
& song.

       Grant me that strength
he who must remain
unnamed

Stuart Z. Perkoff

Selection From *Art Is Love Is God*

The California morning
      is soft & holy
we walk the sky
         like blue birds
turning the corner
      making our bodies one

sometimes like feathers
      falling to the earth
in humble prayer

& sometimes
         I stand against the mountain
& think of pebbles

Inscribed On The Venice Beach Poets' Monument

      I am a man
who stands against the mountain
and thinks of pebbles

Frank T. Rios

SPRING SWING

rain wet
fresh born
the crop seeded
& brite green things shoot for the sun
lite winks on us

i am weak too
new
colt-like skinny legs
wobble bones in the air
tremble to support my own weight

chesty
heart-beat
new word world
springtime satiidy nite
fiddle-stringed knife notes
the wired fingers
box blowin

we seek to speak
to all green thumbs
who look to the sun
& feel the rain in the face
moon juice
partial to poets

the ladys tears   Tony Scibella
                                       1960

*The following is an excerpt from poet/artist **Tony Scibella's** seminal work recounting his time among the bohemians of the Venice Beat scene, specifically Stuart Z. Perkoff*

The Kid In America

stuart brought me to thebeach.   he brought me here.   we met at miltons birthdayball   cholly brought him from thebeach & it was a gd time at miltons likealways being percussive w/miltons old 78's of hamboneblues & we were funny   he liked a couple of the daubs i'd daubed bythen & he give me a lookme up if yr ever at thebeach & oneday i did going to get cholly to front me & stuart wuz there   we stood in chollys room looking at chollys painting which hadgone off the canvas on thewall to the walls around theroom doorframe windowframe back to the canvas on thewall & we leftthere talking &
hardly stopped
          i had a 1/2hearted paintingjob delivering supplys had the use of a truck & since my dad was my boss i was loose hourlylike him wanting to see me straighten out veteran kickaround school coupleyears its time to settle   i'm spoutin vangogh not a nickel   pollock   themasses   in commyscaredydays my dad knows i'm cracked   i wanted some thing somewhere & cdnot possibly say what it wuz but i heard it in blackbars & i thot art/
                    i started stopping by to see stuart when i had a delivery i'd end the run at the beach & park the truck to walk & talk&talk meeting zen&exivisigist alike   why we came suchfriends we were both at a point in life poised to leap into the void to what?   into the eternal lunchbucket to be snapped closed responsible satisfying all qualms of family as to sanity&worth or   always or   dreaded or   alternate or: thelife! bohemianbabes beware two rootinshootin poetfellers ah no   it was serious considerations to unfold   stuart had his own smallfamily i acquired my own soon after   not simple to balance time&frustration wanting the cutoffs the beach&the babes not saying this of course having highdesigns of mansquest inlife & freedom to.
stuart unloaded boxcars i rolled intermittent ceilings sputtering along in our intentions boundbypaint i taught him how to.   onelesson like: its ezy man, any one can do it & he did.   his color was orange.   we went to gallerys showsmuseum wangled ourway into a vangogh 100paintings at the countymo preview/
                    thru   emptyhalls   we   wanderwhacked   by vincent in bold red so who wd not in the parkinglot scream w/joy exultant in belonging?
                    stuart taught me to write by showing me the pencil. thats how, he sd.   but howlong is the line i ask.   as long as the breath, he answer. & that was my longline. 2 words. short words. stuart called it `the cut-throat gurgle' & he told me patchen & cummings creely & if i cdnot speak yet i wd.

stuart came a long way from st louie thru newyork as a teen trying to crack the theatergame as an actor or director i forget.   as stuart told it: it was a girl in n y that told him he was gd when he read some verse to her & being the romantic of course it was a lady that gives u yr first as it was for me   the firstpiece i did a lady wanted & took & thereafter introduced me as the artist & it was embarass i had to liveup to it.   i am terrible as to dates as when something exactly happened kind of judging by howold my kids are relating inaccurately to time so if i say i met stuart when melody was 2 fine but i dont know howold melody is now it must havebeen maybe 55 or 6 just before <u>the suicide room</u> came out by jargonpress   quite an honor for a youngman starting & this pushed him toward commitment &lipton (who was writing his book & interviewing stuart) gave him a lot of encouragement &being lipton was an `old' published pro-writer: important i know it meansmuch to youth to hear an olderpro in yr own profession say yesucan   go for it.

   stuart flung over the edge & took me w/him. opposites: he was political not joining partypolitical   more anti-pain like: people puttin the hurt on people anti or bookburnin anti   i was a veteran lovedgames of ball & card & horse he didn't i was spade&hondo he was miller&lawrence implied a whole social difference in getting where we stood on thebeach walked thru different schools attitudes of face & nationality

            o ho but not that he hadnt read spade or didnt w/urging dig hondo & look forward then to sacketts down the road   he wd read a christie in an hour voracious & how very hip to reach on thewall pulldown a book & read u a verse just exactly what u were talking about & he cd read from the lung the hair on yr neck standing & women fainted overcome i've seen it   he'd give'em that stare & rumble that thickthroat voice   the blueeyed mortal jimmy called it, deadly at 20 yds

                i dont mean to makefun just remembrance of yesterday & friend but i do think of fun & serioustalk of wife&strife & laffter as utterjoy of life embarking   tumult we lived balancing world&word rollingbennies thru the nite stoned on tide&earth raising arms to sky yes! yes!

Tony Scibella

THE GHOSTS OF VENICE WEST

They are already ghosts
John and Philomene
As they pass
Along the Boardwalk
This highway of poetry and death
Where ghosts and poets overlap
As they pass, the gulls
Ghosting above their shadows
Everything's haunting everything
Already ghosts
John and Philomene
Under the ghosts lamp posts
Of Venice West
Their cadence
The breath of sleep
At rest
Lost at the edge of America
Already ghosts
And each poem
Already a farewell
Everything's haunting everything
The sea is the ghost of the world

Philomene Long

THE GHOSTS OF THE POETS
*"Wild Kidney" – improbable English translation for an entree,
printed on a restaurant menu in Kota Baru*

"In case you wondered,"
said the dead professor they had
summoned up with their ouija board,
"In case you wondered, we don't die.
We go to the galaxy in Andromeda."
And he described it, one tedious letter at a time:
Andromeda, a place of immense
and unrelievable serenity;
a bland and sexless, suffocating place
with not a single wild kidney.
I don't believe it.
Like Shelley, Stuart Perkoff was cremated.
I picture his stubby hands curling into fists.
The blackened body bends into
a sort of boxer's crouch.
Stuart's head: beard gone in a puff
at the first blast of flame;
eyes bubbling that had once, perhaps,
seen into me; skull,
fragile as an auk's egg, crumbling;
flaming bits of cerebellar tissue;
ash of synapses across which had once
flashed poetry, some rather fine poetry.
Smoke. White smoke rising.
But Stuart dead? And the rest?
I don't believe it, won't have it,
not for a moment. If he, or if even
the poor and indifferent poets,
are always floating away to Andromeda,
what is left remarkable here
beneath the visiting moon?

So against all logic I say
the alphabetic professor lies.
They are here.
I say the ghosts of the poets
squat in doleful rows on telephone wires.
They crowd the fence rails, weigh down
the branches of the trees. Glumly,
they grub for pennies in the dirty sand
high up at the heads of half-lost rivers.
Some flicker like sad fireflies,
flashing dimly only when we blink.

But they are here.
They are sad, sadder perhaps than when they lived,
but not in Andromeda. Damn ouija and the truth.
They are here.
Do you know what I mean?
Even the barrel of my pen
is full of the ghosts of uncouth poets.
In case you wondered,
they are the wild kidney. They are
the bitter crackling sound I hear
when Philomene brushes her hair.
In case you wondered,
they are the small transparent parasols
all of us stroll beneath.

John Thomas

Transcontinental Bus Trip While Reading Evolution Book

West of Denver
      fossil rodents appear suddenly
            fog & snow, superhighway
Clods of dirt
      reading Hitching on Evolution
            the Central Electric Supply Co.
Watson & Crick, 1953
      crystalline spirals of DNA
            coded info only out to protein
                  molecular "how" of heredity
Schnooky's Cookies
      wire fence
            romantic in water vapor
Baby cries in seat ahead
      Precambrian jump from bacteria
            camping phone next right
                genetic drift in fruit flies
Black on yellow diamond bicycle
      lovers fight
            about their children
Simultaneous unrelated advantageous mutations
      Clear Creek Canyon
            Marcel Schutzenberger scientist says
                "no leaps in nature"
Idaho Springs
      Self serve---no smoking
            Sun races west, into blue sky
130 million light-sensitive rods and cones
      Next rest stop Silver Plume
            system of coordinated variables
Firewood for Sale
      Continental Divide
            Push here to exit

3/89 Highway 80 western states

Richard Modiano

Just a Writer

I want to be Elvis
But I'm just a writer
A tired, weary wordsmith
The apple of my mother's eye
The end of my father's boot
The tender planet of my existence
The death of my innocence
The birth of my ignorance

I just want to walk till my feet collide with space
I just wish for one minute
The world would revolve around someone else

So just for that minute
They could die a million deaths

I fill breath with death on a levee flooded with stolen memories
There on the edge
I walk like Poppa
Footprints in shallow grave

Radomir Vojtech Luza

The Poet Who Beats His Wife

The poet who beats his wife
does so gently,
while he carefully
watches from the corner
of his calculating eye,
the folding-in of her soul
as each verse he composed
to detail his innermost desires
for unattainable women
rolls smugly and neatly
out of his mouth
to the laughs and applause
of a scattered audience.

The poet who beats his wife
doesn't require a road map
of bruises and scars
on the surface of her flesh,
but with an exacting eye
will document the
chronicle of wounds
layered over her heart,
his sadist nature
his unfailing muse.

Marie Lecrivain

Round Shouldered Dreadnought

His eyes reflect
her tobacco sunburst skin,
smoky throated vocals imagine clouds,
seagulls echo through Alaskan wooded
tone forests.

Spruce scented rhymes,
melancholy vantage,
diminished 5ths of whisky
drown hammered thumps,
bellowing thunderstorm cadence
through her sonorous canyon.

He gently reaches around
her slender nodular neck,
trebled fingers hammer
brass rounded nickel chords,
harmonics multiply,
she rests.

Manipulating every phrase
of her rapturous choir,
fondling her total breadth,
his arm brushing against her pearled curve.
Fingers tap on the bottom of her spine,
understatement of disappointment
he is not worthy to play her,
he's just a little off beat
with her surroundings.

Jerry Garcia

TAKIS, My Cypriot Lover

My Cypriot Lover

is probably dead by now.
men don't live long in that
part of the world. there's
always some cause worth the
dying.

My G-Spot

"I never knew,"
he said. in a land of shrouded,
voiceless women, I
cried out, raked my
nails to blood
across his back, arching
yielding
into him, couldn't get
enough of him

he had let loose
a lunatic. a woman who
came at the least
provocation, who
spread her legs,
showed him the mystery.

Oh, the infinite power
of his up-close investigation,
my wetness slathered all over
his smile.

My Regrets

A lifetime later, and sometimes
I still think of him when I cum.

Oh, Takis! Black-haired Adonis,
eyes the blue of the Adriatic.
Did you ever find another like me?
Or did you spend your whole life searching?

Alexis Rhone Fancher

Panty-less at the Annenberg on Saturday Seemed Apropos

I. *Cassiopeia*

Avant-garde in two dimensional
black and white
with a kiss of shiny crimson stilettos
bleeding through a lens
ready to incinerate.
A bicycle chain locked around
cobra-crossed ankles, fishnet
pantyhose stretch thin.
Submission spread across
glossy pages mold girls into women.

II. *Reflections of a Nude Model*

Gazing at almost perfection
is staring down the barrel of
a loaded .38 special

a loaded .38 special
is gazing at almost perfection
wishing to be orchid or child again.

III. *Luminous Transfixion*

She speaks in tongues without uttering
a single word, language is in the eyes,
the anatomical makeup of illusionary grandeur

In her musical movement which
stages the sun as a hot lamp
just long enough to expose luminosity.

Did June ever wonder
who Helmut imagined
when he was inside her?

Panty-less at the Annenberg on Saturday Seemed Apropos previously appeared in *Cultural Weekly*
Apryl Skies

The Deuce of Cups

the black would-be poet told me a story
about his cup in the middle of a forest of cups
and how there was a golden cup
it was *the* cup
and how he found it
and had known that it was not brass
as were the others
and i knew he spoke of another woman
the woman who was half-black and half-ceylonese
who wove spices and spells into tapestries of love
she was his gold flesh beauty with hip-length silken brown
hair. he told me about her as he talked, reached for my
thigh, kneaded my soft darkness and told me i was a
bronze cup in his forest of cups
and cupped my breasts and
his hands worked the bronze, fired it
found it strong yet yielding
he told me gold was much better
but he had lost her
had abused/misused and she had been taken by another
man and so he was content to have bronze
to fill the cup with cum

Wanda Coleman

Narrow Beds

The spare honest lines
of my girlhood intersect
with wood and linen --
Corners neatly tucked
I dreamt alone
with a radio
under my pillow
to ease the nightly terrors
Vampires sucked the dark
Death coaxed slyly
like Southern Comfort

I dreamt alone
long legs became longer
sinew and joint extended
Terror shifted from vertebrae to groin
The womb drummed insistently
Rapists scuttled from street lamps

I hunted boundaries
chanted pregnant lists
of lovers and college lecturers
clocked the seconds
from impulse to scream
slept in sheets of wild control

The demarcation of form --
bed, body, dream --
the weight of cloth
bore me down

There was a limit
a finite space
my body could not slip away.

Laurel Ann Bogen

l.a. suicide blues strung out on existential blanket in the wind

author of my own cliché, descending
a slick timeworn bannister.
holding on by a string, less than a string, to which
a mournful, soft gust could tear connection to
the larger web, tangle
of charred deception
of hostile preempted maturity
of post mortem for youth before life
of forcefed malodorous preconception.
a mournful, soft gust that were it to alter course,
upends root from host,
reveals primary cause, or
splatters ancillary effect,
self evident upon discovery.
irreversible finale, not grand- last thread of
the overcast prism, sow's purse of silken ear.
ear that never heard.
ear deaf to that missed in closing credits.
a mournful, soft gust lopes onto the bloody canvas.
any hope that was, lost
to fateful insinuation. perhaps
to coincidental fate, clinging
to the ornate web i wove, sailing atop
silent wings of fly by night to
another's aura on the nape of sour breaths.
none, no hope, had ever been found in
the stuttering tripe.
i, me- author of cliché
bleeding intractable self pity,
parched for serotonin or
a best left unenunciated offramp.
counting the ways to
leave this city
right where she found me
so as to quiet us both into
a false sense of security.
the closing horizon's lullaby
to back-alley self-deceit,
unprepared to jump the train
until spikes & ties
issue the platitude, as if
it were some challenge or dare;
ashes to dust, if only to save time
as inveterately bloated santa ana blows

a mournful, soft gust thru still, broken night.
dystopic epiphany birthing its dream
under corrupt searchlight
ensuring graphic detail
of even vaguest blur. waking to
reality, naked truth tautologically harsh
despite rainbow wrapping, eventually
revealing spider veins, futile struggle,
before it all fades to black.

Danny Baker

dream journal entry #3

a crowd had gathered
at the base of the building
some woman had crawled out
onto some window washer's
scaffolding,
she must have been
at least
24 stories up
she was dressed in an
old night gown
and she was screaming
screaming and cackling this terrible
manic laugh…
though I couldn't hear
what she was saying
she was obviously hurling insults
down to the curious group
of people down below…
she had this crazy hair
that was billowing around her face
and there was something
wrong with her face
her mouth was covered
in a dark ring that looked like
charcoal or old blood

after some time…
the crowd began to lose
patience
and began yelling at her
why don't you just jump
you crazy bitch?
yeah jump!
soon it became a chant:
jump jump JUMP JUMP
and suddenly I was angry
with her…who did she think
she was?
freaking out up there,
making a scene
and fucking with the
morning traffic…
I was tired of it…
why didn't she just
jump, and get it

over with…
what a fucking coward,
frustrated…
I decided to join in
on the chant
and just yelled up:
JUMP!
and just like that…
she did…
fucking leapt out of
that scaffolding
and came flying down
at us…
at me...
and she was still
screaming
and laughing…

about half way down I
could just make out
what she was saying….
don't leave me!….don't leave me!
that's when I realized
it was my mother.
and she was
looking
right at me
with tears streaming
down the side
of her face
and then she hit
the ground
and split
the sidewalk
and my heart wide open.

Dennis Cruz

Selections From *Art Is Love Is God*

In all the quiet moments
when god looks away

I sit under the light
the knife & Buddha
to my left
the book open
after a long day
with the naked page
gives me hope
that this day will end

& the prayers will kiss the blood
still on the Buddha's knife

Frank T. Rios

THE SUICIDE ROOM

I have within the head a room of death:
brown walls (the death of spring), a vague breath of
seasmell, a ring of knives of every kind
circling a centered mat.
                             The failing lives
to be accompanied by flat drums,
dovecooing horns, plucked strings.
                             The supplicant comes,
he sits upon the mat. Attendants bring
paper and pen. He wills his philosophy
to the world and binds his eyes. And blind he dies.

This is the room I go to when my mind
extends no further than its hidden doom.
I weld the music and the knives into
a power over deaths.

                             I leave the dead
within this room when I have held power
for long enough to go beyond the point
beyond which one cannot possibly go.

Stuart Z. Perkoff

Cenotaph of the Swallowtail
for Vera Jayne Palmer

… all is unfinished and the unending is only just beginning…

This is no fairytale,
no Hollywood dream.

In the still disarray of morning quiet
even birds bow in silence,
perched upon tight wires,
wings folded in reverence,
their sky a threshold
for which they need no key.

Frankincense burns sweetly at the altar,
no name engraved.
They are here to be certain,
dressed in black rain and foreign tongue
smoke spins a web of memory
and gunshot glory.

This is no blind plea,
there is no banquet here,
no black tie affair.

White roses mark tombstones
scattered like black beads
War stories and suicide,
decapitation beneath modest stone.
Blood mistaken for wine
stains her ivory silk.

This is no fairytale,
this is where castles
crumble into the sea…

A place of rest for vessels;
an abandoned shipyard
of static and still beauty.
Chiseled marble visage.

A swallowtail nuzzles names
never to unfold like new wings;
only memory emerges
from a warm chrysalis.

Every grave is a cenotaph,
a hushed indigo epitaph
carved into sky.

Apryl Skies

SOMETIMES WHEN ALONE

Sometimes
when alone
the wonder of your lips
caresses my mind
and soothes the troubles of a violent world
where bullets pass through life
from a trigger finger crying for love
whose path gone awry
set the stage for mass killing
and human atrocity
sent into thin air as smoke signals
from a smoldering gun

Sometimes
when alone
the soft touch of your hair
draped across my body
protects and shields a delicate heart
from the rampant ills of society
where a breath of life
creates an arched rainbow of awareness
across the blood red sky of humanity
falling in a blanket of ash
from the bones and skin of a smoldering gun

Sometimes
when alone
the sound of your beating heart
into my ear brings the comfort
of a child nestled against a mother's bosom
whose milk has flowed throughout
the history of all creation
whose love poured from nipple to mouth
devoured any thought of weaponry
whose child reared never needed a gun
whose child grown into maturity never needed war

James Berkowitz

THE NEWS TONIGHT

says nothing about Nigeria, 300 girls
missing from their school to be sold
into slavery or married before they're 13
years old. At 13, I had an English teacher
who thought herself a poet, had published
a book of sentimental ("sweet-smelling blooms,"
etc...) verse. I loved her. I wanted to be that
tightly girdled 1950s woman who could write
anything she needed to, even "heavenly
aroma of eternal spring," as crappy as that
sounds to my adult and jaded ear. The news

tonight ignores Nigeria. Those girls are somewhere,
kidnapped by men who don't believe in women,
education, writing, the living risk we breathe when
there's a chance: a lucky birth into a place where
even women held together by their "foundation
garments" had the literacy to set themselves on paper,
to inspire my ignorance toward possibility. I would not
marry into slavery. Dear God, whichever God is near us now,

send the Angel with a flaming sword who swoops in to avenge:
Michael. Yes, send Michael to vanquish wrong. And then,
forgive. I am not flawless. How can we not wrench ourselves
away from our own sniveling woes to cry for wounded souls:
the Boko Haram -- those violent ones who hold the girls
and won't let go. The girls themselves. May there be freedom.
May there be mercy. Mercy? That may be clichéd, just like
"sweet-smelling blooms," but, shit, it's all I've got.

It's everything right now.

Holly Prado

Mural on Panos Pastries' Eastern Wall

On the west side of Winona Bl just south of Hollywood Blvd,
a young man paints a mural.
I walk by, look at it, return & ask the young Armenian man,
"I know the 100-year anniversary of the genocide is this year,
who is the female figure in the mural?"

"The woman in the center is my grandmother."
There is a tape over her mouth,
1915 in large numbers on the tape.
"On the left is a memorial with smoke coming out"
that goes across the mural.
It curls up into a large cloud of Armenian faces, figures.

In front of the woman is a mountain, she cradles it.
"That's Mt. Ararat; it looms over Armenia, but it's in Turkey."
"On the left are trees that turn into crosses with people;
the Turks put naked women on crosses; & then to the right
are crosses with no one on them."

"To remind people of the genocide."
"There's money between Turkey & the U.S. & they won't use the word."
"There's art & then there's art."

Tears came to me as I was walking east on Hollywood.
Lately, I have been mourning the death of my sister, but I have not cried
until now. Tears for the million & a half Armenians killed by the Turks;
tears for my sister.

Harry Northup

Selections From *Art Is Love Is God*

Long before now
I could write
how much I missed
the long road to the colors of the poem
glittering with passion & mystery

She used to whisper "leap leap"
the poem is in my mouth
when you kiss me
you will wonder
the wonder inside!!

    Yes the tongue is jeweled
    laced in stone

    The boy knows
    when he grows
    he will like a jeweled poem
    bring her wonder!!

~~~~~~~~~~~~~~~~~~~~

The surreal poem
      Kisses
The black stone…

The rose falls
      A thousand years
Into her hair…

Last nite
everything
came true…

inside I'm just
a boy
pitching pennies
against the wall

Frank T. Rios
~~~~~~~~~~~~~~~~~~~~

Cybele, Let Down Your Hair...

and give me a reason to hold on,
please, give me an impetus

to escape the lightning flash of grief
that bisects the heart in two,

the children who slay each other
in the sandbox, and memories

rewritten by those who
don't want me to be free.

Marie Lecrivain

Unnoticed

She waits just beneath the surface
Behind a veil, within a crevasse
And you would never guess she's there

Her eyes become one with the moonlight
Her claws are sharpened for the fight
And the world walks by without a care

CLS Ferguson

MIRRORS ARE SLEEPING WINDS

Mirrors are
Sleeping winds
In this glass room
Its window
Dreams into frost
Hours after hours pass
I sit before it
Death
Swinging in slowly
In her pleated black skirt
The night, black
As patent leather shoes
It is palatable, the sounds
Of the newly dead
Grinding their teeth
In a grin of relief
Too soon to be ghosts
Too late to speak
As I, neither fully dead
Nor fully alive
Sit with them
Upon their marble lakes
I do not feel
Their marble kisses
Upon the poems
Steaming on
My marble lips

Philomene Long

Margarita
PLACE
Mexican Restaurant

The Night Grows Teeth

The night grows teeth
needle visioned
through curtains
under blinds
the women undress
unroll stockings
they sit painting toenails
a subtle mauve

The night grows teeth
a tribal dance
the steady pads
of footfall and drum
he stands at the window
chest bare
to listen
she circles his back the
night grows teeth with
soft sucking kisses he
unclasps her beads

Grit-song
clench-song
the night grows teeth
it lurches like a madman
it holds you down
it silences you with its heavy hands
it opens you up with its hot breath
it dares you to dream

I know about the night
I whistle myself into waking
I've fashioned arrowheads
from stone
the night grows teeth
it demands retribution
leather straps
and burnt flesh
horsehide
batwing
I paint my face
with yellow ochre
I carry a knife between my teeth.

Laurel Ann Bogen

gritted teeth ground to stumps

gritted teeth ground to stumps
beneath jaws clenched in
fitful sleep.
everything is war.
hungry taxidermists dreaming
of cyclists screaming
the common language
of road-kill.
an empty space
on the mantle,
or on the wall
between portraits
of long dead
relatives.
lips curled in
expletives hurled
at an ambivalent
sky.
a vast silence
coming like a tidal wave
from the edge
of all we can remember.
is death
really
what life's
to make of us?
from sin to id,
from id
to self?
I'm so sorry
for your loss,
words tossed
into the snake pit
of mourning.
the hierarchy of being
pitted against
the philanthropy
of seeing
deep beneath
the underbelly,
oh but the sad
remaining
lost and forever
wandering
the vast wilderness

of understanding.
reporting
from the edge
with the nile
shrinking
and the light
abating…
constellations
shifting
by the trick-light
of the moon.
we were young
once,
dared to die
for the cause
of reason
retching
from too much
fried food.
drowning in
a gluttonous pool
of hardened
arteries
and laboring
hearts.

Dennis Cruz

Every Assemblage

there is no cure for this…

there is only the thing you need to breathe in
the receptacle for your tears
your laughter
your mindful assertions

there is no cure for what makes your day livable
there are only
notes like medicine
drip drip dripping melody and rhythm
and something odd
something perhaps African in origin
that marks just the slightest hesitation
the merest distraction
in the storied arc of today's sun
a blip that virtually no one else will even detect

there is no cure
there are only the words that mean other words
there are only the colors that inject unknown definitions
into your skin
there are only paragraphs
that reach up
wrap punctuation around your throat
make you beg for air
for release
for endurance
for every molecule you have ever encountered
to vacuum out your frailties
and use them to finger paint the night sky
with constellations of gravity
with clouds of solidity
with silent ripples and insanity that is really joy

there is no cure
just ask van gogh, he knew
ask lorca, he sang it
ask hemingway he ran with it
ask strummer he spat it
ask the homeless guy pissing patterns into the sand

there is no cure for the things that hold us to the earth
that seek us out in our starry arrangements
that give us wings

give us roots
put stars in our ears
and glissando in our eyes

there is no cure for the first time hearing that collection of sounds
no cure for that hour staring at framed glory
no cure for that dog-eared escape route
not for us

for us
the pluck of the tightened string
puts wind in our sails and our lungs
the swirl of texture and hue
is the jolt that moves corpuscles from one chamber to the other
the precocious organization of syllables
staves off the dismal and the depreciation

for us
there is no cure
indeed we do not want one
we every day draw these plague sheets
up around us as armor
we every aria drop into something like the divine
we every assemblage of wood and parts
sing loudly into the silence
dance sometimes hesitantly but always with adventure
into unknown orchestra pits
we every wicked dark room develop our answer
our gift back
to the world that tolerates and glistens us
to the common elements that are anything but in our hands
in our lungs
in our fevered nostrils

for us
we only need know
not *if* someone will listen to our song
but that there is someone else
who absolutely needs to hear any song

for us
that is the disease

David McIntire

Selection from **On Higher Phlogiston Current For Aime Cesaire**

"...the internal contradiction, extreme tension, and complexity in Cesaire's imagery place him closer to the late poetry of Artaud than to Breton."

-A. James Arnold

Your spirit
entranced by the scope of entangled scorpion moons
rising from the height of flooded monsoon trees

as if
in a pre-intestinal era
you consorted with the essence of trilobites
with the essence of in-fluvial lions
like an utterance from the cells

there existed as concurrence
a blinding amniotic
a lethal testing juncture
which you summoned like a bell
calling
the first grave dogs of Kemet

& these grave dogs
bearers of wounds & theocracy
gave you
the first glimpse
the first hieratic magnification
of the way the stars were shifted at your birth
they gave you
the first ardour
the first nomadic dressing gowns
in which you appeared
magnified out of ether..."

Will Alexander

hermetic overload w/ a ten foot couplet & art is theft
for gail wronsky

traipsing around invisible corners on a silent night,
there's a dream coming to fruition so it then may die.

exiting on a lark w/ no leg to stand on & questionable
wing—there's ample space tho none for agoraphobic.

dreaming up quixotic fantasy in atypical mythological optimism
runs amok in hyperbolic parables. on the downside of a steep

incline i find no shortcut thru bowels of status quo, putty-face
spawning-salmon pining for tepid waters. corralling clowns

to capture mediocre epiphany in closed caption for white liberally
impaired freedom fighters, adroit of striking skill—a bubble set

to burst whilst the injured walk off decades' nettled hangovers &
sharp snap of reeds wielded by malaysian bamboo marionettes

to negotiate nightmare in an impossible dream & incalculable
potentiality sprints headlong into quicksand ditch.

fighting off the inevitable insurgence w/ existential insurrection.
learning to spell why as luck eludes me in a bus lane.

traversing a moat of crocodiles on benzos & jack. the tight rope's
hangin' loose, safety net—a silken star. & she's coming right at me—

Danny Baker

Thoughts, Acrobats

From the acrobats, long taut thoughts
and their costumes of tiger stripes or fire.

All day I felt them performing--

torsos entwined, or
the hard work of a Rolla-bolla balancing.

One time their high flight got a kink in it--
could have been a lonesomeness
or was it simply a forgetting.

Their sci fi leaps
their lacquered hair

scary as wayward dogs and "entertainment."

Thoughts, acrobats,

swoop on.
You keep me in such antic clover.

Gail Wronsky

The Lid of a Jar

Pictured on the cover of the Museum of Natural History magazine
Is the lid of a jar

Except for the magazine's title, the whole cover is taken
Up by the face of a young Egyptian noblewoman, drawn big
Against a vermilion background

This is the lid of an urn used in ancient Egypt as a container for
The viscera of corpses to be mummified

The noblewoman has a wig and
Her eyes are of obsidian and quartzite
A glass image of the
Sacred serpent had originally been attached to the forehead

Her loved ones left behind would have assembled before her
To mourn this dead woman
Some would have prayed, some would
Have waved incense censers, some would have made funeral
Offerings of great price

The lid of the alabaster urn would
Then have been removed and her internal organs
Gently placed within

What memories would have stirred then in those
People as lid met jar?

Richard Modiano

IN THE OCEAN OF NOTHINGNESS

Wading into clean, wrinkled laundry,
my ironing board's a pier
with buttoned-down barnacles.

The water will be warmer tomorrow.
It sloshes around my ankles
as I walk between sticky pilings.

Hip-deep, I finish the sleeves
of my third shirt, lean back
and float on crescents of disbelief

until I sink. A little background noise,
even in these depths, makes illusions
more believable to anyone gazing down.

I went for a long swim last night
between two tiny continents.
The entrails of a transparent fish

swayed in mordent harmony.
Near dawn, it spoke: "I am this universe."
Its gills rippled like buoyant silk.

In the Ocean of Nothingness first appeared in *Upstreet*, subsequently in *Beside the City Angels: An Anthology of Long Beach Poetry*, edited by Paul Kareem Tayyar; & thereafter reprinted as a broadside by Rick Lupert, June, 2014.

Bill Mohr

Impossible

any metaphor is a distortion
what therefore is true?

it is impossible for us to ignore the literal meaning of words
even when the literal meaning produces the wrong answer

and the people who get to impose their metaphors on the culture
get to define what we consider to be true

what therefore is true?
a mobile army of metaphors and anthropomorphisms
a sum of human relations
that becomes poetically and rhetorically intensified
metamorphosed
and adorned
then
eventually, after long use
becomes fixed, canonic and binding

any metaphor is a distortion
what we consider to be true

truths are the illusions
that we have forgotten are illusions
they have become worn out metaphors
which have lost their power
to affect the senses

any metaphor is a distortion
poetically and rhetorically intensified
what we consider to be true

a mobile army of metaphors and anthropomorphisms
what we consider to be true
and adorned
becomes fixed, canonic and binding

truths are the illusions
that we have forgotten are illusions

what therefore is true?
when what we consider to be true
is a distortion

any metaphor is what we consider to be true

what therefore is true?
a mobile army of distortion
impossible for us to ignore

David McIntire

Lingering Discontented

You brag about the drawn bow
Before the slaying of a single Cyclops,
You speak of sacred runes, their secrets,
Before hanging from the Ash Tree,
You roll away a stone from the Lazarus tomb
Before laying hands on a single wound.

I am Lilith's husband and she is never coming back.
I gaze upon an apple in the garden, imagining the taste.
Twilight; the first of the figurative rises, then falls.

Before myth and legend, there is the wind,
A breath above the foam, a shivering leaf,
A time when earth beckons to the knees.

I must pray. Will greatness come to me?
There is nothing monumental to propose,
No earthquakes, no Calliope on a spring breeze.
No tropical hurricanes in the far latitudes.
There is nothing special in this room.
I sleep here. The existence of one more dream.

Can I still be a fable in a buried scroll?
Can my life become my generation's allegory?
Can I be the hero of your fairy tale?

Behold such grandiosity born anew.
I want and I want and I want some more;
Such desire our fuel… civilization and its lingering discontented.

John Lavitt

OVERCAST, CHANCE OF REAL RAIN

Man across the street: black pants, black shoes,
black hoodie sweatshirt tight around his head.
A monk? Grim Reaper? Or maybe
just a guy who's going home before it rains.

His long-legged rush, his fast intention to prevail --
always my question: Who's real, and who's the Other?

Scrim: theatrical, a character itself this veil between
my understanding and my ignorance, striding like
the man who makes me think about those cop-car/
criminal fast chases down the freeways -- their eternal
TV coverage. I watch; I want to know how desperation
flings itself against some ordinary night, no matter what the price.

Having an answer to The Mystery shouldn't be my business;
yet I came into this world desiring everything, grasping
and weeping. I knew, I know, I'm sure there leans a door
behind the solid dark. I know the man who's
striding past me has to show his face to somebody.

Holly Prado

Radana's Supermoon
    after Jorge Luis Borges

You must know that you are immortal.
That your vast circle can accomplish all.
You offer so many faces, but keep one
we never see. At the dark side, your lips
recite an alphabet of stars.
And your emptiness takes the night
in search of a mirror.

Keep talking. It's only a matter
of time before you get an answer.
Even though *there is such loneliness*
in that gold. Recall that kiss.
That one kiss that made you first turn
toward the world.

Lois P. Jones

Call

I rest as the day warms, hear
through closed windows the faint repeated call
of the fog horn, three miles away. It warns off
sailors but I don't know who those sailors are,
and it warns me: You are not in charge. Your
children can be taken from you,
your life ended over and over
before it is over. Listen,
it says: A voice. That's
all you have.

francEyE

END OF DAY: WHITE CANDLE

Within the flame, there's
message, but I can't spell it.
White flowers, too, profusion.
More languages than I can learn
before I am, myself, completely silenced.

When weary Moon goes to Her other world,
vigilance becomes mortality's surrender,
its fast dissolve: Wax on the table; wax slithering
along the candle's own smooth sides. I'm
not attentive to the stubborn table's wood.

The message finally is "melt." The flame forgives its burning,
forgives my match. Here's truth from hidden Moon
and from the whiteness, from Tuesday's useless
conversation: Everything is better written down.
Each waxy drizzle marks vocabulary we have always
needed. Within the flame, there's death;
there's swift reward: unseen but heard.
Unheard but memorized.

Holly Prado

Pattern & Light
    for Rebekah

I remember the day, I loved you already…

No one has ever sculpted us
into marble or Medusa

Only fine *memoryblur* of pattern and light
dancing off walls
celebrating glorified silhouettes
unaware of beauty beneath the surface

But Hope sees something more
a thing of light that moves beyond
spills over oceans
of darkened shadow-cast framework--
barren meadows of misstep

Someone in a field with open eyes
reveals there are dandelions…

Sees vision in *lensblur*
saturation and color-corrected memory
a rough edit, salvation…

Fucking forgiveness for once…

In the archway of impeccable light
refraction reveals itself
an impressionistic painting
of what strength wishes to become…

Fragrant rose
sharp black thorns
halo adorned.

Apryl Skies

Ciudad de Los Angeles

they speak of angels often in the place where I was raised
everything was named as if it were a holy attachment
connected to an angry god that sent his forsaken
battered children into a desert wilderness
next to an oily seashore of lost teardrops
that was the summer playground of the
wealthiest kings who laughed in their
drunken debauch of every sacred
name ever given to the home
of the unforgiven meek
who lost every inch
to the greediest
one percent
as they bought
it all up
for nothing
only to rent
it all away
for
everything
the angels
had left
for them
forever &
forever more

A. Razor

California
NOIRIST

L.A. River Lullaby

It's 2:06 am
I can hear the sounds
of a distant train
as the constant passing of cars
drive the 5 Freeway
alongside the L.A. River
heading north
and heading south
going to places
called home.

Home for me
is not a place
with walls
windows
and doors
where framed photographs
are placed on mantles
over fireplaces
and lined hallways
or embedded
in refrigerator magnets.

Home lives in my heart
and in my breath
and in the unsaid exchange
of knowing glimpses
with loved ones
and kindred spirits
ignited by
the reciprocity
of trust
kindness
safety
love
and the generosity
of a spirit
that goes beyond
material items.

Beyond
coaxing words
and gestures
for planned outcomes.

Beyond any exchange
of anything
wanted
or needed.

Home is not
the room
for the life
but for the life
in the room.

Home lives
in the conversations
that our souls
are having with each other
without words
where truths are unspoken
with an unconditional love
that rings louder
and with more power
than mere words
could ever express
with an emanating
everlasting
unstoppable
force.

Home is anywhere
the heart thrives…

as the passing cars
on the 5 freeway
get quieter and quieter
until all I can hear
is the distant train
and the unspoken words.

Iris Berry

Untitled

there will come a day
(poets will build this custom)
a day will come
with changes.
we cannot even consider them
without being thought mad.

        our caution
in disguising them as artistic
fools no one.
                        (every rose pollinates. even the stupidest
                        know this)
no matter how beautiful
in the center of our roses

is the stink of
another thing.

Stuart Z. Perkoff

Voice of the Voiceless

I am the voice of the voiceless

For the men locked down in these California prisons, I speak for them

For the ones locked down since 1975 and it's 2014 and haven't had a visit, I speak for them

For the ones that have to stab their best friend over prison politics, I speak for them

For the ones that will never know the scent or touch of a woman, I speak for them

For the ones that will never set foot on free soil 'til their demise and even then don't set foot, I speak for them

For the ones caught in the web of this bounce back system, I speak for them

For the ones that are free in prison and are imprisoned when free, I speak for them

I was once silent but now,

Hear me speak, hear me speak.

Rolando Ortiz

HEAVY DAUGHTER BLUES
for Yusef Komunyakaa

the t.v. is teaching my children hibakusha
i am in love with a dopefiend who sleeps under freeways
my neighbors are refugees from S.A.
and i speak negrese

the source is promising to terminate my train
of thought. the postman has put a hex on my P.O. Box
when my mirror cries do my pupils dilate?
i put my dial on quiet, my ears are gaining too much hate

> *i went to the clown show*
> *disguised as you*
> *you did not*
> *recognize me*

i dream i dream i dream
pass the pipe — please

put the gold in the shredder
Vietnam has taken Hollywood in helicopter blades
& kliegs
(let's arrest the runts)

i always withstand other people's hopes & desires
until they doublecross me. then we clash

i have proof that the culture of the biz-zi-ness man
is disappearing due to his inability to produce
one perfect realm of solitude into which
sanity can be delivered

when reading all those thick tomes written on God
it should be noted God is caucasian

the first stone shall be the last

the voice of our millennium is a niggah junky
gagging on stage
to heart-felt bass & trombone
pissing rhythmically in his jock
snot running into his forbidden funky os

now that machines have finally taken over
we get into something serious
like art

i have my one-way ticket
to the moon
i am inculcated with the dangers
of incriminating love

after riding the desert in her '63 cherry cad
she uncovered herself beneath the sphinx
rut on her breath

the t.v. is preaching my children hibakusha
i am in love with a fuck freak who
lives in my alley

the constant preoccupation of a sphere
is in traversing the Möbius strip

i throw the symbols. i make reverberations

myth/my girlchild and me
cackle joyfully in the kitchen
as we make cookies
for the party of the world

Wanda Coleman

Moonlight to Water
For my youngest sons, Ruben and Luis

Ruben recalled the day I brought mama
and his baby brother home when he was six.
In the back seat of the car, he said,
was an Asian looking child,
hair sticking straight up on his head.

Chito—short for *Luisito*—looked this way
because he's part Raramuri and Huichol,
but mostly all universe.
Ruben must have wondered about the galaxy of stars,
bird songs and stories that had been dreamt
to fashion such a boy.

When Chito arrived I'm sure he knew—his world would never be the same.

Until then, Ruben had been our only child.
To mom and dad, he was the screech
of car brakes,
a sigh to a bad joke,
the glove to our ball,
and now this—a bewildered boy gazing
at a sweet-faced earth child
wrapped in a light-blue blanket.

I asked Ruben what he thought about his brother.
Eyes gleaming with a six-year-old's clarity,
he answered: "Oh, I already knew him—I saw Chito
when I was in mama's stomach."

I gave Ruben a look I often offered
in reply to his amazing observations.
Somehow, though, the statement rang true.
His younger brother was in the wings,
preparing to part, the next one,
patiently abiding his turn.

As they grew older, Chito followed his brother's
every move, entering wide-eyed
into Ruben's dense sphere,
sharing the same music, games, imaginings.

Ruben never hurt or exploited him,
as older brothers often do.

The boys connected from the start,
like hummingbird to flower,
like breath to poems, like
moonlight to water,
brothers since the womb.

Luis J. Rodriguez

LITANY FOR PEGARTY

Pegarty, consider the possibility
in the trillion, billion, million
light years since the beginning of
this universe and I don't know precisely
how long afterwards it was with you
that I was once the same person
the very same person – only you
in this immensity of space
as well as time
I shared a womb
only with you
none other and I knew you
before you took your first breath
Pegarty, and you were the very first to
put your arm around me
in that same womb it was your arm
that consoled me
Pegarty, it was you who heard my first breath
and ever since we breathe together
for this, especially on our birthday
I am grateful, yes
in this expanding universe
of five billion years (is it?) none but you
Pegarty, with whom in this expanse
as well as others unknown to me
I floated timelessly in that womb where
we kicked and slept in the warmth
in the darkness from which I kicked you
out into the world at ten minutes to
ten o'clock on August 17, 1940
St. Vincent's Hospital I kicked you
out into the blazing light so that your cries would
be the first sounds in the trillion, billion million to
the trillionth, billionth, millionth power of all
sounds ever emitted, yes
so that yours would be
the first sound I would hear as
I emerged from the darkness and
now in my darkest hours it is always
your arm I feel
your voice that I hear

Philomene Long

Just Do It

When I ran like a child into my mother's arms
When I felt her hug like the softest and tightest pair of arms
When she looked at me with those dark hazel European bulbs
When the love she gave far outstretched the pain she suffered

Then and only then
Did I know my own strength
My own capability
My love of humanity
My need for people

Then and only then Did
dead skies grow And
Lazy Susans sprint

Only then did wicked nooses
Find their way around my neck
In payment for what I had been given
In reward for having gotten through so much
There was more to get through

There was academic poetry in all its cold uncanny warmth
There was jaded you and jaded me
Def Poetry Jam in its television performance mode
Three minutes for half an idol

And why because fame Equals
quality these days Celebrity is
akin to importance

And so somewhere down the line
When the hand meets the keyboard
And the mountains touch the cockpit

Will the imagination once more be stirred to
Vacation alone

Radomir Vojtech Luza

In Being My Father's Daughter
for Daddy, Silverio Duro de la Vega June 12, 1928 - May 8, 2007

Because laying on the bare hardwood floor
is too gentle and aesthetic and still
does not offer that masochistic solace,
and because crawling under the bed to weep is
only an instinctive feral urge,
it seems the next thing that might do it,
that may finally satisfy and replace the urge
to cut my face with an exacto knife,
would be to break something,
smash all the windows, burn my guitars,
topple the piano, club the TV to pieces,
slash my sofas like the D.E.A.,
break all my dishes
... and etc.,

Still, playback of the sequence
"madness as medicine,"
only proves that out of every single object in my home
I can't find one fucking thing that can present to me
the perfect punishment,
here and now
needed so badly...

Daddy & I were deemed "wild eccentrics."
Infamous, the both of us from L.A. to Manila.
We remembered being peacocks in a past life together
we never gave a shit about what the Family thought.
la la la...

I could jump off the roof,
I won't die but it'll hurt.
I did not kill my Father, but someone else did.
Yet I am guilty, after longing to be with him all these
lost but hopeful years.

Guilty...
of not being at his side to
kiss his mouth at his final sigh,
breathing in to catch and
hold his fleeing ghost inside me,
for just one moment,
for the parting in this lifetime,
our spirits' last embrace
here and now.

Instead, I was fucked up,
drunk and jacked up in Hollywood,
when I should have flown
straight to Luzon days ago.

I was the worst daughter
he was a worse Father,

which is why I was his favorite,
and why every man
I've ever truly loved
is exactly

Almost Him.

Yvonne de la Vega

A Place Called "Well"

Now they wish to introduce me
to a place called "Well".
Can one reach an appropriate destination
by swimming in the sand with boots on?

I see my way to Well through
someone else's window.
Well refuses my imagination, will
not be tried on the way fantasy
might a prospective lover.

Well waits on the shelf of some dried goods store
all chewy, brown and wrinkled sweet.

Well floats by my left thigh
like some slippery silvered fish.

Well mocks me with its steady job.

Well marries in a white dress and
bears three smiling children.

Well rolls around like a glass eye that
watches me but doesn't care.

Well lines tiny shoes in two straight rows,
starches laundry, washes faces,
feeds the dog, packs school lunches,
throws birthday parties and cocktail parties
and never drinks too much wine.

Well produces home movies of family trips,
wraps presents for under the Christmas tree,
cooks breakfasts and dinners and
never burns the roast.

Well gets wrinkled from meetings with teachers
and greeting the guests.

Well rests contented in the afternoon,
cries old blue tears at borrowed weddings.

Well sighs, smug in the evening,
boasts photographs of grandchildren.

Well haunts me like an hourglass

on the mantle, running out of time.

And how will I know Well?

I don't even know enough
to ease down in its rocking chair
wearing down the floorboards.

Well sits in the sitting room.

I dance on the rooftop,
dangle from a telephone wire.
I am far from Well.

Jennifer Bradpiece

Y YOU ARE MY X (or ode to nothing eternal)

We would wander these streets in search
of the perfect defect—my turquoise heart—
the ruin of this city. Each car accident,
police siren, helicopter searchlight
compelled me to praise you.
I once fell in love with your solutions,
the orgasm organized with a hygienic Windex
bottle blue association of fire—nature's way
of clearing away the old. I loved you on a cold night
alone
burning away our sheets. Now, I fixate.
I consume myself with the turquoise woven line across
the unnecessary wool socks smothering my toes.
In these clean moments I find the unknown winter,
the element
a life populated with possessions
sum totals
things you
left
unnoticed
like the ember of shadow on the floor
bleeding through the slats. Or
a hemorrhage of sporadic protests—
I've become the schizophrenic down the street
eating out of the dumpster like a birthmark.
Today, I hate your voice when the heater clicks on
and even more so when you say
life is not an imitation
but a response
a cry
a song
a god of silent laughs.

Kari Hawkey

SZYMBORSKA
1923-2012

I came home
Wednesday night from class
and Lori was ensconced
like a caterpillar in a cocoon
on the bed, watching a movie on tv
about crazy people who fall in love
and break china.
"Szymborska died," I said.

She reached for the remote and shut the tv off.
The room expanded into that quiet bubble we experience
when we shut off the tv.

She looked at me and said nothing.

What was there to say?

A friend dies, a
poet dies,
poetry lives on:
There's nothing
you can say.

It's like turning off the tv,
and their passing
fills the space of our lives
with all that silence.
A balloon of being and nothingness,
a reduction of existence into a series
of appearances, overcoming those dualisms
that have embarrassed philosophy for centuries,
and replacing them with the monism
of the phenomenon.

I put the clipboard
I still had in my hand
on the dresser
and began to undress.
Then I got in the bed and lay beside her.
We still hadn't spoken.

Szymborska was gone.

We just lay there for a bit, in the silence,

not sure who would break it,
not sure whose turn it was
to turn the moment
back into words.
You need a poet at a time like this,
and the poet was gone.

There was a small crack in the ceiling.
And a tiny cobweb in the corner.
Later, Lori'd probably get on a chair
and with a tissue
wipe it away.
That was her job, getting
those little tiny spider webs
gone before they engulfed the house,
our lives, the planet. Don't
worry, dear reader, she's on the job.
You will be safe.

"What's my job?" asks Lori when she's nagging me.
And I repeat the mantra: "To take care of me."

But for now, with Szymborksa's passing
still blooming into silence,
the cobweb would have to wait,
the crack would just have to bide its time.

Such a long silence.

Then I thought, fuck it.
I reached for the remote,
and clicked the tv back on.

There went a teacup.
Crash.
There went another.
Crash.
It was good to get back
to a semblance of the world,
all that love and passion,
all those broken teacups.

Jack Grapes

A Star-Crossed Supernova Hastily Written on a Diner Napkin

You are hundreds of miles away again, pining.
Or is it farther than that without expectations?
No doubt you are happy in Anonimityville.
You are cut off or blocking out the world.
Or is it just me that you are casting off?
Did I or you or both of us deserve it?
Was 'it' worth reimagining yourself?

I ask too many questions, you always say.
You are cryptic and wear it vaguely like a veil.
I don't need specific answers, per se.
Just hints, allegations, and shadow puppets.
If you're going to break my heart again,
leave me the duct tape, glue, and whiskey.

I can't read in the failing light.
I need a sign telling me to stop.
I hear your voice from the other room.
It coos to me from beautifully bound notebooks.
But you aren't in the other room, inspiring me.
I know now that was just a walleyed what-if.
You don't shine for my city anymore.
You have become the hidingest monster.

Won't you embrace my tangible starlight afterburn?
My second wind is imminent and electrifying.

The calendar flips over and we come up for air.
I don't want to put a limit on this bittersweet longing..
Here I am again, dashing and jittery like Morse Code
but without any urgent message to get through.

Won't you free my heart galloping in my chest?
I used to quell it but now shun all soul cages.

I murmur long forgotten secrets at the walls.
In splendid indifference, rain pelts the aluminum siding.
The lush and dank cacophony renders me inert.
It's a choir I never asked for on 24 hour energy pills.

Won't you belay your wanderlust tonight?
I will share the wine if we forgo glasses.

Recite it to me like your favorite summer chorus.
Illuminate this wanton, wintry scenario.

Tell me the story of us.
The epic Might-Have-Been.
Of how it was never the right time.
Or that we were on polar opposite trajectories.
Or that neither of us could wait for the future.
Not when the present was burning like paper Mache
excuses in the desert with only gasoline to drink.
Not when edible words were all we had.
Not when you kept writing star-crossed supernovas on
used diner napkins and I stopped reading, already full.

Eric Lawson

STUCK

I'm stuck in Beverly Hills
not interested in the riches of Stefano Ricci
or the vision of Persol

I am a flyby
waiting for the 720 Express
and looking for a place to pee

Hardworking tourists
take photos of everything famous
helping to keep everything famous

Long legged models strut by
and being thieves of attention
they don't carry cameras

A skinny old vagrant slips passed the police
to pick through a trash can
for the lunch of his life

Teens walk for blocks
never putting their phones down
as if the world were one long Oh My God

I grow increasingly agitated
If birds had to use public restrooms
they'd explode here

Jack Cooper

PSYCHIC DEFENSE TRAINING FOR EX-LOVERS

When I walked out on you
You came up inside me
Infiltrated my body with your strange feelings
Trussed up my struggling energy *chakras*
So I had to follow you around like an emotional doggie
Except you could walk through walls
And I had to go around the buildings

That day I pulled on
The lower half of my dreams
And headed out – Hollywood Boulevard
Within and without you

It didn't work
I had to kick off traces
Of sleazoid hound-dog faces
Of fellow citizens
Baying dangerously near
Giving advance notice
Of my own decay

On and on I walked
Into your thin ether
Leather and guitar stores reeled
Like drunken sailors
Snakes flowed out of my stomach
And into the stomachs of old friends
Whose sideways glances showed me
I am sucked out from within
Dry as the wind
Nobody told me
The human heart
Is a cactus

Doug Knott

SUNSET WALK

Is this nameless pain, insistently loading my back, what pushed me on my evening stroll tonight? I think so, since I advance in a sort of numbness, step by step, as if against resistance. I am listening to a Beethoven piece, over and over, earphones stuck in my ears. I marry the moods of the music, its intensity and release, fight, catharsis and glory. Four times in a row, but I'd go forty if needed. Yes, repeating the cycle until each cell surrenders... until my scattered fragments align, recomposed in a system, an organism… that I am supposed to be.

At that point, my pain is not gone. It's absorbed, though, at rest.

In the meanwhile I've walked several miles without a trace of fatigue, deepening into the texture of town, seeking new corners and angles, facades, roofs, doors, windows… Or else flowers, trees, people. I have found them, and each new discovery hit me with a pang, a blow in the stomach, perfect mixture of marveled joy and sharp nostalgia. Like it always happens. Each house, always, talks to me, projecting the shadow of a life that could have been. And I long for every house, for every life I haven't lived, as if I had lived it instead... as if I could feel both the presence and the loss of them all.

Every garden strikes me with unique botanic details, bringing back my early wonder, untarnished, at the magic of plants. In the same way, I incredulously stare at the beauty of each woman sitting on her front porch, in the lassitude of this evening hour. Old women, poor women, dressed casually and still with natural grace. It's the laced edge of a sleeve, the shape of a cleavage, the contrast of a belt or a simple ring. It's the way the hair falls, the bend of a neck, a nape or a wrist. It is a crossed leg or a swinging ankle, a lose sandal with painted toenails peering out. Artists didn't honor enough this daily display of splendor. Every new frame pierces me with a longing of I don't know what.

From a lit interior, only partially shaded by a curtain, a man gestures at me. He is up at a second floor, still I see him quite distinctly. He must be undressed, although his lower body is invisible. Clearly, he's inviting me in. There is no vulgarity in his enticing attitude. Nothing disturbs me. I have the feeling of having seen this before and I might. Isn't it part of a known scenario, isn't there every night, every few blocks, somebody who gets naked alone then spies out, looking for an object of sorts to ease his or her lust? One way or another? I sure understand. I know about that solitude, that anguish of the flesh, so banal yet hard to cure.

Suddenly, I am swept by a wave of desire that I haven't felt in a long time. For that skin, which at a distance feels smooth, anointed, almost plastic like. At a distance I think I can smell it, not transuding sweat still or the pungency of sex, but cheap lotions and soap. I wish for the touch of it, for its consistency… that must be compact, dense, almost fake, like a doll's. I am sure. I perceived it in a glimpse. This man of age undefined, bold and thick, reminds me of my father. I desire him and I desire that room. A cheap room, because cheap are the house, the garden, the entire town where I live.

Yes, I know this town, but I never walked here before. On this street: I savor its taste of exotic, due to unfamiliarity, of course. It dead-ends against a massive stone gate. It's the graveyard.

Well, my mood could have brought me nowhere else. But it's late, the place is closed and that's just as good. A part of me is dead anyway, tonight: no need for inspiration...

A part? Which one?

I'm listening to Beethoven again. He sure died, long ago… but he keeps me company, he's the liveliest thing around. These notes, dulling my pain, are all I hear.

Plus, sometimes, the labored rant of my consciousness, stabbed, transpierced, imploring, remembering, weeping, denying. Trying to dispose of corpses, but hopelessly.

Toti O'Brien

I Wanted Him

I wanted him:
This guy who sliced meat into cold cuts at Encino Deli—
bologna, salami, pastrami, belly lox
No socks, no underwear
Crisp white t-shirt without stains, careless and low slung 501s
Careless, before it was kool

I wanted him:
This cross between William Katt in Carrie
and a Dickensian parish boy
I'd been sneaking looks at The Joy of Sex
in my parents' hidden cabinet
and he became the person I'd picture it with
He was larger than life, surround-sound
He looked like he'd been around and around
Peter Frampton, Roger Daltrey, Robert Plant;
every Seventies rock icon rolled into one
and even behind that counter,
he was Someone

I wanted him:
Through the chocolate phosphates, the bialy specials, the Halvah bars
--and was pulled in by the way he'd stare at me
He'd stare at me through my entire meal
and it made me feel
Seen

I wanted him:
For I was used to Mama's Boys;
the price of their toys, their bragging rights, their allowances,
their five and ten year plans
Where were the cowboys on my brother's flannel pajamas?
Where were the lumberjacks from "Here Come The Brides"?

I wanted him:
There was no hiding it
My mom had taught me to fall in love with love;
not where to find it, not how to work it
LOVE as the only answer
Her bible was a book of poems
called, "There Are Men Too Gentle To Live Among Wolves"

I wanted him:
Because when I would try and imagine the men in those poems
(the ones my Mom seemed to long for)

I wondered: What was wrong with them?
Why weren't they stoned and reckless?
Those were the kind that I leaned towards

I wanted him:
As he'd stand on his feet for hours at a time
while the neighborhood shlubs whined that the Nova was too salty
I knew he was deep beneath the drugs; durable, too
and the only other non-Jew in Encino besides my best friend
Yet the more caring I was, the less he stared

I wanted him:
To press me up against the old Encino oak
but when I spoke, it was clear
I was a virgin on the pill, still waiting for the right first
My bible was a book of poems
called, "My Song For Him Who Never Sang To Me"
The men in those poems weren't gentle or reckless,
just hit'n run absentees

I wanted him:
To deliver bags of bagels to my house, comp my egg creams,
drink Club Margaritas from the same can
He was the only man who could pull the Tel Aviv out of me,
straighten my curls, make me Norwegian like he was

I wanted him:
To give me a ride in his VW bug that during a flash flood
had rolled down Laurel Canyon by itself,
crashed into a series of parked cars and survived
Even with his hands in the pepper-beef, turkey breast,
lean strips of tongue,
it was 1978, I was fifteen years young
Had a brother who beat me with words and his fists
and I saw this post-modern Oliver Twist as my way out
of the Valley

I wanted him:
To undress me in his car and teach me the secret to dreaming so I
stole all my Dad's quarters, cashed them in for dollar bills, took
the RTD to the Whole Earth Marketplace in Woodland Hills and
bought him a glass bong
And then
I shaved it all into the shape of a heart,
read The Sensuous Woman (memorized the tricks)
and I asked him to take me to the Styx concert

I wanted him:
So I didn't tell my folks that after the show
we would go back to his apartment in Tarzana
where I would bring not only my mood ring
but my new favorite record,
"In Through The Out Door" by Led Zep
It was common knowledge that if you took a wet rag
and rubbed it against the album's inner sleeve
it would leave behind the black and white drawings,
transform them to permanently colored

I wanted him:
As if being in his presence
seemed to heal me from convention, certainty and excess
It was nothing less than awakening
to muffled speech that revealed itself in reverse
Back-masking and lock grooves were all the rage
and I was underage then,
decoding subliminal messages from album covers,
imagining older men as lovers,
navigating firsts

I wanted him:
Even as it hurt in his bed, I focused on what I could see:
His hair, golden movie star ringlets that smelled like Flex shampoo
His hands too, away from the meat-cutting machine,
far more serene than one would think
His body, sinewy and covered in freckles
"Kisses from God," Mom called them
I had 'em too

I wanted him:
Though his girlfriend stared at us from her senior portrait
so he turned it around, made her face the wall
As I recall when it was over, I wasn't invited back for a year
What's become clear is that for decades
I carried him along as blueprint,
and in those I've loved there has always been
a hint of the grown-up orphan,
the waif-like fable boy groomed on the street
Who knew his touch would unseat me?

I wanted him:
Still
So I'd try things out on other men
Some who signed their lives away on me |
Let me steal their wild for free

The Butterfly Flick, The Dog and Pony Show
Afraid of the slow-down, the love-scene
I'd try things out on other men and think,
"One day I'll come back and show you what I've learned"
I didn't care that he wanted nothing to do
With me

I wanted him:
All because
When he'd stare at me from behind the counter
I felt seen.

Susan Hayden

My Love For You Is Whole
  (*but slips through the cracks like rain through a leaky ceiling*)

Our love started like a secret
Tucked away underneath rocks
For protection.
But like the ocean
The tide pulled our love,
Crashed it up onto the shore,
And scattered it across the sand
Like shallow treasures waiting patiently
For the idle hands of recovery.

We are born beneath the stars
And grow from the sun.
We will cut our way
Through this earth time
Like a glacier,
Fine lined and
Even around the edges.
We are smooth, baby,
And our love is a glass window
With a picture of a future
We are to make,
Future paths that we should
And shouldn't take.

We are sweet as wine
And bitter as all the drugs
We couldn't shake.

You are the eye
And I am the cell of clouds
That swarm around you.
Together, we are storm.
We are furious
and beautiful.
We can take and break
Our own destiny.

You and me, baby,
Are king and queen
And I want to have a tribe
Of legacies that
Erect like statues
And fall like rubble.

You and me together,
We will survive like we always do
Because we make it
through this lifetime.
We do because
We have passion
And we are hungry.
We will live forever
Because we can't stop
Despite the hell of mockery,
and the constant struggle
To keep the dim lights on
In this darkened town.

We got the love
And we have the hour.
We keep the dead close
to give us the power.
We are me
And we are you.
We touch those around us
And take what they give.
We are a sharing nation
Waiting to begin.

We have love!
We have love!

And I want to sing this song
On all the trains and busses.
I want to skip with you
Through all the puddles
And splash our love around.
I want to paint it on every wall
And take ads out in the paper.
I want there to be more
Than our art driven by pain and anger. I
want to bust this love like a sunspot And
send gamma rays through personal
Ozone layers and infiltrate people's brains.
I want to orchestrate
A love parade
And run through
The halls and coat them
With sun filtered dust,
Iridescent and magic

Like you baby,
Like us.
We are the makers
Of this phenomena
And it is our responsibility
To let the record be heard.
It is our responsibility
To play the music,
Play the music,
Play the music...
So that we,
Like the others,
Can feel the rhythm
That keeps us snug in the
Brilliance of our emotional freedom,
That keeps us safe in our small speck of heaven,
That keeps us close when we seem so far.

We are
The spirit of romance,
We are!
And nothing can keep us down...

Annette Cruz

MY OWN PRIVATE RESURRECTION

—after Mark Hartenbach

i'm thinking about a love i have never owned,
drenched in the madness of a man who has never
let me love him, nor has he fully loved me.
he is as close as an argument. he is as close as
the dirt under my nails. he smells of dark closets
and babuskas mopping the floors of The Tzar. he is
the Mecca of my pain, bearded and lust-lidded,
stooped by lechery and time. he never sleeps. as
morning waxes he counts my dreams, barks at them
in his guise as wolfhound. our survival has dwindled
down to "at any price." my pride and my shame ride
me—those twin witches—as i fight the dust, the debts
and the rude distractions, as i move to shake God from
heaven, to win the means and right to live on without
him, i am consumed by a love i have never owned.

Wanda Coleman

Forgotten In The Outer Reaches
for Dennis Cruz

There's a heavy cadence looking for the lyric. Truth expanding to the heavens where spurious underpinnings relegate responsibility to black edges of the galaxy instead. Rocking humanity in furious backbeat fronting the one man lineup. Screaming agony into the ether as if to say I'm here, like it or not, which can be a coinflip when supplicating to unmerciful norms. Sleeping through nothing is nodding out on whatever assignment to scorch keys with sunbursts of dead skeletons. Burn burn burn that fucking house down. Riff those chords through splintered hearts. They're coming together, vowing retaliation as one though there's always an excuse. Don't go there. Just don't fucking go there. Don't go down that path of venomous nettles rattling anticipatory for an open wound finally not of my scales. Bloody battled introspective carnage-fear ain't' something you could begin to provoke. I've already locked it in my reflux. Repealing amendments to failing constitution is girding the trellis until its construct is no longer subject to vulnerability in historic storm nor minor brush-up. Running high in size big, creeping to another space. Space and time. Era where if it could only start there, the finish might prove itself proof positive that history repeats. Blanketed by emotional stability is a bit tipsy. Unadorned with bloated canopy is catching all the cats and dogs dogging across open plains with several hundred heads and a cantankerous steed clicking rollicking incantations with flat reprisal. West of the Miss eating up void for the word it circumambulates in a song of doves doing dirge covers while ravens strike evil on unexpected victims. Spinning off charts without as much as a legible cleft seguing to next in creating a non-sequitur which can't make any friends. Bare bone exposed for terror of poltergeists in clown suits reviewing roadside freakshows behind one-way glass. Broken never stirred is taking it back for resolution by absolution requests yet won't grant his own wish. The Church of Me is hissing- spitting new life into old beats looping repetitive. Nothing changing, but for timing belts, allowing one more for the road or tree in front of your house. Returned from outer reaches to earth carrying a torch too big for one to handle in theory yet there's always someone fucking up the curve. The rafters again- the rafters shutter to reverberating basslines. Acerbic basslines. Gratefully not all peak performance is purview of Asians. Nothing wrong with 'em which is precisely the problem as simple equations are solved in three blue notes. That rompin' hardcore is jazzing it north. Knocking heads with its clone. Alighting. Setting the world aflame. Next the moon. And that fucking Asian kid with the perfect score.

Danny Baker

So That One Thought Lives

Back then my dog was ocher
and a green rain skewered.

In my head were two acrobats:
a twist of day and nighttime in the cranial tent.

Which gasp was it that I heard?

Then yesterday you called.
I was at an environmental rally
thus choked on
destiny and self-esteem.

At the windmill of my heart
two guys you knew blew
through the bone door.

Sullen, drunken, their wishes
numb to a bite.

Later, wearing sky,
you and I, we enthralled
our justice brothers.
Those humble simples.

Money, we said.
I was half awake.
Mobs and the clouds have gone off
into their dewy lairs
with tightropes.

Gail Wronsky

Kitten With A Whip

more destination than place
Los Angeles remains a
shifting landscape of
water and sand

mercy has little to do with life here

nor is this city the cruel, friendless,
kitten with a whip that many
would like to believe

make of it what you will
these eviscerated roads are my river
lit by the constant final flash of fame

a first and last chance city with
as many ways in
as there are out

some doors give you breaks
others leave you broken

coyotes heckle the anxious laughter
of countless gods
hawks surf the invisible wake
of tireless angels

we are homeless, home and
homeward bound to the distractions
and could never deny our stories
inked in blood

a phone rings
and excites the air
inside this wig rodeo
of love and death

a cancer of some undying hope
swells within the bones spinning
the myth and music of all things
possible under this
bleach blonde sun

S.A. Griffin

My book got drunk again last night

My book got drunk again last night
and wouldn't stop talking at me when
I thought I needed and wanted some sleep.

Shut up book, I tried to say
but my book jumped up off the floor and
landed on my chest and began crying and
laughing and pulling at its jacket and
art work and publicity blurbs.

It yelled that if I didn't read it
right now it would kill itself.

Well, I was saving that whiskey for
a good day, book
I said, very disappointed in it.

My book said it was sorry
that it just got bored laying around
on the table while i was out and
saw the bottle on the sink and
well emotions can be cruel sometimes.

I made a pot of lousy coffee and
tossed it all over my book which
got it sober
enough to crawl back
into the closet with all the other
books that were bitching about how i
should get them read.

I think then I finally went and got some sleep
I could have been wrong.

Scott Wannberg

MOBTOWN

Standing on the sidewalk, outside the Terminal Bar near the corner of Fifth and Vermouth, Manx pounded another nail into his coffin. It was midnight. Everything shook loose in this town 'round midnight. Inside, Charlie Barnet was blowin' a fat, rich sax on the juke and it was spreading like molasses across the empty dance floor. It was prom night for the hawk.

Outside, that tired old melody lay down on the sidewalk and waited for the clop-clop of death to reign up to the curb and take it away from all this. This delicate moment was lost on the crowd of late-night losers and literary stumblebums, who shuffled past on their way to Palookasville. He wasn't sure where Palookasville was, but he'd heard that it was down by the Harbor, somewhere between Wilmas and the 'Island'. Judging by the burn-outs that he'd seen thus far, it wasn't *anywhere* that he'd like to be.

But then, he was never where he'd like to be. He was always somewhere he'd wished he wasn't. So it goes.

The street was littered with the leftover scum that the cops had failed to rehabilitate in Night Court. A skinny hombre named "Frito" circled around him like a shark with the seven year itch. He sniffed the air for that first sign of fear. Manx avoided eye contact, knowing that he'd have the first dance with Mr. Machismo if he did. Hombre malo. *Muy bad medicine.*

Manx caught a glimpse of his face. He looked like a weasel. Manx had known a guy down in the harbor, once, who looked like a weasel. Was this his son? While he pondered this, the weasel moved off, still hungry. He had an itch that only murder could scratch.

In the distance a dog barked.

Someone leaned on a horn, impatiently, as if they were taking an unscheduled solo. The city pulsed and throbbed to the rhythm of the night with a horn section provided by the intersection of the one-ten, one-oh-one and ten-west. The City of Commerce was taking an extended drum solo and the MTA provided a Bootsy Collins-bass line, as it bored through the guts of the city.

Manx thought about that, about how the city was being gutted by a giant subterranean mole, even as he stood on that street, with the denizens of the dark. Even as the little dramas unfolded behind the walls of the buildings around him, even as someone begged for more and, elsewhere, someone begged for less. Even as Frito was scratching his itch and an act of revenge was being plotted. Even as the moon cycled slowly overhead, making its way back to an early retirement trailer park at Paradise Cove, even as the sun was gassing up for that long pull over the Banning pass.

He thought about God and the atomic clock, about the universe expanding like the air escaping from a blown-up balloon, suddenly released and whooshing recklessly around. *If this was true and the universe was really like a balloon, Manx wondered what would happen when the air ran out? What would happen to the balloon? Worse still, what would happen to us?*

He let out a long, low whistle of amazement.

It was midnight and the night was young.

R.D. Armstrong

Scott Wannberg in Florence, Oregon, July, 2010

People who have long dropped out of sight are visible here.
Scott's the only poet in town;
Being Scott, he's secure on this spiderpoint of coast.
He is very large, but his
true presence is light.
Bright wings of morning
in the cage of the body

Off the main road, he pays low rent and lives
Next to a police sub-station he waves hello to.
I sleep on couch cushions hopscotch on the floor.
We talk the old stuff: SA's mac & cheese
Dutton's deceased bookstore, the endless forever Carma Bums,
How Dustin Hoffman leaped up when he heard
Scott was waiting for him with books! "What? Scott waiting for me?"
    Yes, Dustin jumped for Scott - and Mr. Dylan, Jackson Browne
    And all those movie people with the flagship names
    Always sought out Scott
Because he was already an angel,
and lifted them up
despite their weight of fame

Because he was a Colossus of Soul,
Flitting on heavy feet between the stacks
Finding first the books you want, then the ones he wants for you.

I remember the carbo-mad burgers and fries
At Early World eatery across the street in LA and
The recent year Scott couldn't sleep,
like he was stuck inside his own TV.

Time to eat! Ding dong!
Always a ceremony of delight,
The action is down at Thornton's family restaurant.
We walk there, Scott truckin' that oxygen tank
Behind him on its little mouse wheels.
Transparent breathing tubes corral his nose.

He takes 'em off once we're inside, oh yeah -
3 waitresses serve him 3 meals each sitting.
They fawn over him, Scott, of course they do!
We all can't help it. He's the consummate consumer.

I'm proudly here as "friend of Scott,"
That much-littler guy on the other side of the table,
visiting from that tormented giant LA Scott's from,
and these folks have only "heard of" ...imagine that!

It's so local here
I'm wearing a big white bib, too, like Scott,
Oh party down! Here comes the food!
Biscuits, pot roast, salad, mashed and those twin
Wedges of pie not long after.

To offset, post-lunch exercise striding with big Scott feet
10 times around the parking lot...
I thought he was doing well –
What a surprise this COPD he's got
Pulled some briny rip-cord in his lungs, even though
His weight's down and he talks like heat-lightning –

That's why I can't figure why he just blew off the personal skin,
And tears come out of me
Like spray from the boiling ocean only a mile away.

Our conversation veers on bat-wings between
corridors of books, expands
at the speed of light --
Towers, bungalows, apartment buildings, cities of words,
Then suddenly all seen from above
Amid constellations slowly twisting in brilliant cosmic dust

In his apartment, we burrow into the stacked books.
I leave with an armload he's just ploughed over. We
Argue both sides of the 1846-48 Mexican War.
He says how some local kid he befriended
and even saved from suicide, ripped him off for several grand on a "loan" –
  No need to collect that now.
  And no need for suicide.
  God does it fine without our help.

Sure, the tombstone crowd is waiting in the wings,
And the virtual world is hungry for more lambs from Scotty pastures.
  But he's left me stark awake on my desert island of mortality
  His poetry marks my forehead like a track-meet of ancient bards,
  His spirit flashes by like a huge wedge of apple pie,
  streamers of ice cream flinging flavor;
  Desserts of Valhalla

That's after the rare steaks of love and
words you served up for so many years,
Scott, and your friendship,
More precious than an evening repast with any god
Or heaven I find in menu or holy book.

Doug Knott

Where To Find Me During Office Hours

I'm in a department of squeaky wheels
Ears plugged with fire hydrants, so I can hear myself think
The chair in front of my desk does not serve as a floatation device
So I'm left to float on my own—a solitary cloud
Downed in my war against mediocrity's atrocity
And this is the office they gave me
So that I could inspire young minds to blossom
In the faraway fields of forget-me-not

CLS & Rich Ferguson

Fear Moves To A New Town

Manx sat across from the La Salle, enjoying his coffee as he opened his mail. The morning sun was doing its best to cut through the chill of early winter. It was not very successful. Every so often, someone (probably some drunk) would let out a scream from across the street. It was natural. Life is a truly scary proposition these days, and the shock of living it would make the most sane among us cry out if we hadn't been conditioned since birth to do otherwise. As he contemplated this (and the swirls in his cappuccino) a youth, of passing acquaintance, sat down (uninvited) at the table and began to rant.

"Truth is a broken mirror. Justice is an empty box. Intimacy is a suicide note. Desire is an empty shot glass."

Your point being...? Manx thought.

Was this really news to this kid? The world was neither safe nor sanitized; yet every time you turned on the box there was some government stooge trying to convince you otherwise. Likewise, every time you went out there was some goon preaching righteous indignation from a makeshift pulpit. Or some kid who had just discovered that life sucked, preaching to the choir at some poetry 'reading' or in some alley where the 'chronic' burned and spoiled dreams mingled with spilt booze. He wondered where these people had been? How had they missed the decline and fall of practically everything sacred?

The kid was on a roll now. He knew it and Manx knew it. Trouble was, he wanted nothing to do with the kid. The kid brought out a fear that had plagued him for years. A fear which he had learned to suppress by ignoring it. A fear that had gone unnamed for years: homo-phobic. *Not as in* homo*sexual* fear, but as in homo-*sapien* fear.

He looked at the kid. He wished he could make the kid disappear... forever. He wondered what would happen? Could he get away with it? Would anyone notice? According to the kid, no one gave a damn if he was ever heard from again. Manx drifted into a murderous daydream of doing vile things to the kid (just to show him how bad it could *really* get) before dropping him head-first down a mineshaft out in the Panamints, or maybe, over by Pinto Basin.

"Truth is a handful of dirt. Justice is the open grave."

A scream punctuated this statement. Manx lurched forwards out of his chair, his letters scattering like bystanders at a drive-by shooting. His hands clutched the kid's throat. It was soft and innocent like a Harp seal. He choked out the words as Manx brought down the club.

"Beauty is getting what you wished for... whether you like it or not."

"Too true, too true;" thought Manx.

He was long over-due for a change of scenery, anyway.

R.D. Armstrong

Tax Season

I've been trying to write a poem about the men standing in front of
the tax preparers office at Parthenia and Woodley

dressed as the Statue of Liberty for two years. Every day I drive by them
on the way home from dropping my son off at pre-school.

They're holding up a sign that says *Get Fifty Dollars Now* and
spinning it like the marketing department just joined Cirque du Soleil.

I make that sign with my fingers that means either *Satan,* or *I Love you,*
or maybe just *Rock and Roll.* I'm not sure which.

But I make it every day, hoping they'll notice. It's a hit or miss.
Some days, depending on who's in the costume, they avoid eye contact,

obviously thinking this is the kind of person who might orchestrate a home invasion.
Other days the sign spinner catches my eye and smiles as big

as a buffalo that's twice the size that buffalos should be.
Yeah he get's it! he thinks. *You know why I'm here.*

And I do. It's only a couple minutes 'til I get home, and as much as I want
fifty dollars now, I could just go to the ATM. Plus, I do my taxes online.

But I want them to know I'm okay with them. That I remember the time
when I was barely one paycheck away from standing on a street corner

dressed as a national landmark, spinning in a circle and hoping for
a bread crumb of acknowledgement. I get it.

I salute you with my Satan fingers, oh human Statue of Liberty.
I love you. Let's rock.

Rick Lupert

GOD IS A LEFTHANDED CHEESEBURGER

If God is a left-handed cheeseburger
It's a prefabricated laminated bovine wafer
draped in Kraft pre-sliced processed cheese food
dripping with Best Foods mayonnaise
nestled between two melt-in-your-mouth Weber's buns
trembling in the clenched fist
of a born again right wing reactionary CEO
as he shouts,
"Take!
Eat!
This is my body!"
Then shoves it down the corrugated throat of Lady Liberty.

Good food, good meat, good god let's eat!

Lynn Manning

Ubiquitous Freud

S.A.: *Faster Samurai Swimsuit Gunfight, Swim, Swim, Leap*, the greatest, gunslingest, grooviest, most gut wrenching gastrointestinal three minute and twelve second western omelet ever made! Starring Ubiquitous Freud as Liquid Chance the swimming pool that women loved to lap, Rock Hardsoft as the fastest impotent gun in the eastwest, Bikini Ghostdance as Sybil Sunburn, Vanna Tanline as Gams Gotcha, Lucky Smoke as the slow burning lone cigarette bad guy Vapor Stinkwell, Velma VaVoom as the Tee Hee Triplets, Linger Lamour as Naked Bathing and special guest star Stretch Your Dollar as Sticky the Lounge Chair. Written by Roger Dollarsigns, directed by Corman Nobudget with musical soundtrack provided by the Johnny Electric Shoestring Orchestra. An AIP, Absolutely Independent Pictures, surrealease. Don't miss this one!!!

SCOTT: Ubiquitous Freud was born Natty Kumquat in Brooklyn. He was the son of Kinetic Kumquat, the famous mesmerist barber and Nifty Bohunk, the Apache fan dancer. Liquid Chance is indeed the role of his life, written expressly for him by Aerosol Lip Sync, and Rock Hardsoft told Enter Detainment Tonight that he was proud to work with Ubiquitous on this demanding film. Aerosol Lip Sync gave Roger Dollarsigns full credit but it's a known inside Tinsel Town fact that Roger writes best for anyone but Ubiquitous.

S.A.: Well, Ubiquitous Freud had spread himself way too thin during the making of *Wet Dreams May Come*, the biopic starring himself and Carl Hung, the guy who invented the Dreammaster and had originally said no to an earlier version of this script, but when he had heard that Vanna Tanline and the many faces of Sybil Sunburn had signed on, he just had to do it! Yes, it is also true that Aeresol Lip Sync shines as Sunny Doo Dah Dayplayer in the sweet roll of a lifetime, but honest to Buddha's belly button, the Tee Hee Triplets in fall down walk on just steal every scene they aren't in! Truly amazing piece of film that is medium rarely seen at any BBQ, but fortunately tonight, the sauce is with us!!! Luke, I am your cheeseburger!!! Help us Obi Wand, you sell the meanest dope!

SCOTT: Ah, bikini girls with machine guns– nothing like the old sex and violence mix that has made so many countries great and small at the same time. Alas, I am like that cat without the kitty green, and so the titles of the movie that was once in my mind remain obscure, like that object of desire I once saw, with my friends, with just one last, tantalizing, lottery ticket. Alas.

Sunny Doo Dah Dayplayer just won the Neville Slurpp award for most cogent screenplay...the Tee Hee Triplets turned into nymphs and Carl Hung was seen on the Dreammaster at the gym and almost had a heart attack from having the Dreammaster on full velocity!

S.A.: Ah yes, but in the second act, Hung is saved by Suzanne Summer Vacation with her Buttmasterbator!! Hung and Suzanne are brilliant together for the last time first time, Dollarsign's dialogue is nothing less than brilliant, and I do mean, less. Les Ismore plays Father Knows Less (typecasting, but whatcha gonna do? Guy's gotta put food on his table). Anyway, the dialogue is simply stunting!

Hung: Hi.

Summer Vacation: Smile when you don't say that.

Les: As I was saying...

Summer: You weren't saying...

Hung: Exactly!

Unbelievable!!! And if you act now, you could be nominated for the Golden Brown award. Call before midnight, our operators are sitting by. The last ten callers will get absolutely nothing, so be the first to be last and win small time. But really, time is running out, so any time will do.

Of course Natty Kumquat become very famous later in life as the author of *The Air Conditioned Condition* and *Nexus, Sexus, Plexus, Who's Got The Erectus?* And Mesmerist T. Barber would go on to greater fame as well playing psycho killer Sweeny Floyd, The Demon Barber of Mayberry. He won several awards that never existed and retired shortly after he died, never to be heard or seen from again except in this short clip where only his voice is heard, altered to sound very low and guttural. That's his voice as the African mask at 1:54 burping, "Faster Samurai Swimsuit Gunfight, Swim, Swim, Leap!!!" How about that theme song as sung by Shirley Bassomatic?! And did you catch Irene Ryan's Daughter blowing kisses poolside? Wow!! Even backwards, it still spells relief.

SCOTT: Aquarius wanted to let the sunshine in, but owed the sunshine 3 months back rent, and Sunshine's attorney Nolo Con Tinted Ray said Aquarius would simply have to chill– pizza delivery man was the shaman of all pizza delivery tribes in the northwest.

S.A.: And lo the tribes did cross the barren land of Ameirgo, I go, we all go! And the clouds burst farting ice cream, which melted over all things and God burped and said, "Excuse me, while I touch my thigh." And his only begotten daughter was born, Rock Well, whom he later renamed, Raquel, and did she ever!

SCOTT: Clouds Burst went to gastroenterology guru to probe his tendency to fart. The gastro guy said if he was set on farting ice cream, he could at least offer the galaxy a wider variety of flavors, as apparently the 2 main flavors that Clouds Burst farted were tutti frutti and chocolate chocolate chip, which in a way, is semi-redundant. It's getting difficult to access the thigh unless you have a Stare Master.

And here are some salient moments from this monumental undertaking...

>Rock Well/Raquel: The beatitude's altitude shouldn't cop an attitude.

>Clouds Burst: Would you like me to fart forth some tutti frutti in your face, Rock Well/Raquel? A pessimist mesmerist shouldn't desist but consist.

And JLo, the tribes did shimmy across the James Darren Barrens and Amerigo wore day glo oh oh no no no.

Hello, welcome to Hip Herbie's High 'N Happy Fart Mart here in the tantalizing township of Tumult. Here we have every known style of fart known to fartologists all over the world. Our trained staff can decipher olfactory fact from myth!

S.A. Griffin & Scott Wannberg

Meander in the Melee

Blood for poppies is the standard fee around here
No one seems to notice that the inflation will
drown you without a moment's hesitation

I don't get it
I'm not an outright dunce
I can walk a straight line in the dark

Bombs are exploding all around me, numbing me
I don't think I'm supposed to be doing this here
I don't have a plan to get out...or was it back in?

I don't want this
I'm not sure who I am...nesia
I can't see my feet in the absence of light

Have I stumbled into a battlefield in a past life?
Do I even believe in all that Tarot card bullshit?
Do I have anything better to do than ask questions?

Don't answer that,
you vicious other me
You sanctimonious turncoat

You left me here to brush shoulders with obscenities
But I will find my way out of the dark tunnel soon
I will no longer be fooled by lights and loud noise

I will kill the map maker
I will burn the storied evidence
Once the paths are lost to the wind,
everything will be a clean slate again
and
I won't
feel so lost

Eric Lawson

BY WAY OF CRYING

It had been a bruising L.A. day
and I went to bed wondering
if I had said thank you enough
since saying thank you
is like looking up at the stars
the more you see the more there is
and the more thankful you feel
about being part of it all

So I said thanks to Theodore Roethke
(who has more E's and O's in his name than anyone ever)
for his line that I'd read that morning
and somehow missed many years ago
"I long for the imperishable quiet at the heart of form"
That's a thought that lives on
from a poet who died too young most would say

I thanked the woman
on the train home from work
who asked me for a quarter
How often I turn from requests like that without listening
(on the runaway train of assumption)
This time I waited for the whole story
as she smiled by way of crying
from her mouth full of holes
She only wanted to buy an apple
because she was having the rest of her teeth
extracted the very next day
and afraid she might never again
be able to bite the forbidden fruit
I understood that the seventy-five cents
I found in my backpack would be enough
since she must have said thank you ten times

I also wanted to tell my friend B.
how grateful I was that he'd called
and listened to my advice
(When was the last time that happened?)
I had urged him to write a book
on his discordant odyssey in a life of music
I knew the first chapter had to be
the day he discovered his dad's shimmering trombone
in a velvet-lined case in the garage
and dropped his piano lessons like a bad note
to become a horn player

on a path of delayed mastery
as an orchestral conductor
(Was there still time?)
To get him started
I mailed him my notes from our conversation
A friend can help you start something impossible
because a friend can go to the heart of your form

And then there was L.
who sent me an email
saying he'd read somewhere that I'd died
and was wondering what had happened
I joked with him that
being among the dearly departed
apparently wasn't so bad
since we all live forever in cyberspace
but I wish I had thought about Roethke
And I forgot to thank him
Saying thanks makes you forget
we're all supposed to die someday

Jack Cooper

I Wake Up In A Strange Room

I wake up in a strange room. The curtains are drawn and I can't tell what time it is, though I sense it's either very early or very late. I realize I'm in a dingy motel and I wonder where I've left the drugs, probably on the table. I look for a table, but the room is long and there's another room, just around a far wall. This frightens me. I know my mother is another room. I get up off the bed and walk over, hoping to find nothing. I find myself walking down a long hallway I don't remember seeing. The closer I get to the next room, the brighter the light becomes. Soon it's burning my eyes and I consider turning back. I don't think I want to see what's in there anymore, but I keep walking, suddenly noticing I'm not wearing any shoes or pants. Finally I turn the corner and enter the brightly lit room. It's a hospital room. My mother is lying on what looks like an examination table. She is nude. There are numerous electrodes and clamps fastened to her skin. She is screaming. Standing around her are five doctors wearing facemasks and holding clipboards. One of them motions for me to not come any closer. I begin to weep. *Don't worry*, one of them says to me, *the pain she is in, is a necessary consequence of her actions. All this is necessary.* I nod to signal I understand and keep a healthy distance. One of the doctors, the only female, lifts a slender looking cattle prod and begins to shock my mother. Her body bucks and writhes. She screams louder, her eyes locking with mine, pleading as if to say: why are you letting them do this to me? The pain I experience is visceral and immense. *This is not your pain*, says one of the doctors. *It would not be appropriate for you to take this from her, she has earned and it is not yours to feel.* This comforts me and a warm indifference settles over me. Suddenly I feel calmer than I've felt in years. I watch the doctors with a curious detachment. They really start to work her over. Cutting her with scalpels, pinching her with clamps, and shocking her with small white rods. Her screams begin to muffle and fade, as if sucked into some sort of vacuum. This comforts me. I decide it's time to make my way back to the table and find my drugs. I can't even remember what kind I'm on exactly, but I suspect crystal meth is involved. Sure enough, there's an open baggy on the table and two sloppily cut up lines lying next to a five dollar bill rolled up into a straw. The bill has had time to stretch and it looks ridiculously fat and comical. I can feel myself smiling as I reach for it, wondering if I should tighten it or maybe just try to flair my nostrils big enough to accommodate it's current size. I tighten it up and snort both rails, one in each nostril, and take a moment to drink in the miraculous burn. Holy fuck it hurts good. I consider praying and mumble something up into the light of the floor lamp. I find a smashed pack of cigarettes and fish one out, lighting it with some matches I find oddly familiar. Taking a long drag, I wonder if maybe my mom might want one, but then remember that she quit a few years ago…besides, she's got her own shit going on. I figure I've got everything I need, just standing there, smoking, watching the smoke curl up in the air.

Dennis Cruz

A Little Death

each evening
before twilight
before starlight
before the yellow houses
pull their shutters
into themselves

I remember my own
small death
in green and orange
and ash white pills
each beautiful
each perfect
each swaddling my senses
in cotton batting
and antiseptic truth
junkie truth

I have died
these many familiar times
this comfort
pulls my life about me
with sleepy fingers
like a warm blanket
and rocks me
with soft lullabies

no mother could
ever be so diligent
so real
so mine

one
two
buckle my shoe

twenty years of
little deaths have
left me silent and
barren as Mother
Sleep
no longer waits for me
drawing a tepid bath
but instead
opens her starched white uniform
and smothers me in her ample arms.

Laurel Ann Bogen

UNSOLICITED LOOKING GLASS

The Santa Anas had been howling at the tops of their lungs,
Making for one treacherously hot day—
A day when the slightest body contact
Produced pools of perspiration
And tight-jawed grimaces on the buses—
A difficult day to keep cool,
Let alone be cool—
An impossible day to be blind and cool—
Nothing like heat agitated automobiles
And sun-limp palm fronds across the face
To magnify the weight of my white cane,
To leave me feeling repulsively blind
and put-upon by life in general.

As I squeezed through the insensate clot of unmoving passengers
To get off the bus,
I wondered if electric cattle prods
Made good walking sticks,
Or if laser canes could be cranked up
To *light saber* intensity.
As I stepped down to the curb,
A woman's hand lighted on my shoulder.
Her voice was a cool breeze as she said,
"I just want to let you know that you are looking goooooooood today!"
Then she was gone—
Taking with her that terrarium on wheels
And the day's oppressive heat.
Gone too were my misanthropic thoughts of mass murder.
My smile was almost decapitating.
There's nothing like unsolicited truth
To clear the path for a brighter day.

Lynn Manning

BREAKFAST AND LUNCH AND DINNER

WHERE I LIVE

at the lip of a big black vagina
birthing nappy-headed pickaninnies every hour on the hour
and soul radio blasting into mindwindow
bullets and blood
see that helicopter up there? like
god's eye looking down on his children
barsandbarsandbarsandbarsandbars
where i live
is the gap filled mouth of polly, the old black woman
up the street whose daughter's from new orleans and who
abandons her every holiday leaving her to wander
up and down the avenue and not even a holiday meal. she
collects the neighborhood trash and begs kindness in
doorways/always in the same browns, purples
and blues of her loneliness—a dress
that never fades or wears thin
where i live
is the juke on the corner—hamburgerfishchilli smells
drawing hungry niggahs off the street and pimpmobiles
cluttering the asphalt parking lot. pool tables in the
back where much gambling and shit take place and
many niggahs fall to the knife of the violent surgeon.
one night me and cowboy were almost killed by a stray
bullet from some renegade low riders and me and
kathy used to go down and drop quarters
and listen to al green, and the dudes would hate
my 'sditty ways and call me a dyke
'cause i wouldn't sell pussy
where i live
is the night club working one to six in the morning.
cigarette burn holes in my stockings and wig full of
cigarette smoke. flesh bruised from niggahs pinching my
meat and feeling my thighs, ears full of spit
from whispers and obscene suggestions and mind full of
sleep's spiders building a hazy nest—eyes full of
rainbows looking forward to the day i leave this hell
where i live
avoiding the landlord on the first and fifteenth when he
comes around to collect the rent. i'm four months behind
and wish i had a niggah to take care of me for a change
instead of taking me through changes. this building which
keeps chewing hunks out of the sides of people's cars and
the insane old bitch next door beating on the wall, scaring
the kids and telling me to shut up. every other day she calls
the cops out here and i hope they don't run a make on me

and find all them warrants
where i live
the little gangsters diddy-bop through and pick up
young bitches and flirt with old ones, looking to
snatch somebody's purse or find their way into somebody's
snatch 'cause mama don't want them at home and papa
is a figment and them farms them farms them farms
they call schools. and mudflapped bushy-headed entities
swoop the avenues seeking death
it's the only thrill left
where i live
at the lip of a big black vagina
birthing nappy-headed pickaninnies every hour on the hour
the county is her pimp and she can turn a trick
swifter than any bitch ever graced this earth
she's the baddest piece of ass on the west coast
named black los angeles

Wanda Coleman

No Mercy

You got no mercy in your hair the way you
shake it in traffic and cause all those
blinded drivers to slam on their bewildered
brakes
the way your eyes invite one to
suddenly snap in half with
the thought of it all
oh, those horrible wondrous nasty
thoughts of it all
no mercy on a stick
you buy it at the corner convenience
no mercy on the tip of your tongue
as the air forces of all the belligerent nations
involved
pile into each other during rush hour
when the sky is full of ornery birds
back talking each other in
strident glee
no mercy in the dark room
where everyone gets exposed
even the quiet ones
sitting there by themselves in
the oh just let them alone and they will let you live
corner
you know how it goes
they say your name enough times
and even you sooner or later begin to believe it is
actually your own
no mercy in the headlines
grabbing you by the throat and the pupils
all you wanted to do was digest your goddamn meal anyway
but you had to go and open up the paper
and the TV turned itself on and spat at you
with bullshit and the pretty anchor people
were all dead inside and
all you could do was fall onto your knees right
in front of it all and
sing
No Mercy in the blood stream
No Mercy in the chorus line
No Mercy in the richter scale
I just wanted to come and play in your sandbox of mercy
I just wanted to climb into a comfortable bed alongside
your wise sacred mercy
No mercy in the playground of nameless children

we are their fathers we are their mothers we
go and rinse them out of our skin but the rinse cycle
never ends
No mercy in the toothpaste
you scrub and brush and scrub and floss but your teeth are
not elected your teeth don't get the lead part they don't
even get a walk on
i came here years ago
for the mercy
i'm sorry, all the mercy is gone
we ran out last night
we have it on order
how long will it take for my mercy to come in
oh, well, the local distributor is out of it
they have it on back order
no mercy school just opened
the tuition nonexistent
you just stand in the middle of the door
and if someone is stupid enough to walk up to you
and ask you to let them love you
all you have to do is either kill them
with a weapon or even worse
kill them with your heart
the one with the sad resume
stuck in it
soon the underpaid legals and the
not paid at all illegals
come and sweep up the mercy
they put it in plastic bags
they seal it so none escapes
they mark it toxic
this sad mercy
and they bury it deep
in the hallow ground
you know where the hallow ground lives
the hallow ground has clean underwear
on and can buy its way out of any trouble
i don't have any hallow ground to throw at you
when i pick it up it burns my hands

Scott Wannberg

INDEX

*Photography

John Macker & S.A. Griffin, 2003

Lorraine Perrotta

www.EdgarAllanPoet.com

Made in the USA
Charleston, SC
04 August 2015